KEN TYLER – MASTER PRINTER
and the American Print Renaissance

O.K. to pull   The Master printer of Los Angeles.   David Hockney 73

Frontispiece David Hockney: *The master printer of Los Angeles*, 1973, 48 x 32 in (121.9 x 81.2 cm), lithograph, screenprint, edition 27

Ken Tyler
Master Printer

and the
American Print Renaissance

PAT GILMOUR

Hudson Hills Press
in association with the
Australian National Gallery

To James Mollison, Director of the Australian National Gallery, who by extending its collection to encompass many of the artists' prints illustrated here, opened up yet more avenues of enjoyment to the Australian people.

First edition

Published in the United States by Hudson Hills Press, Inc., Suite 301, 220 Fifth Avenue, New York, NY 10001.

Distributed in the United States by Viking Penguin Inc. Distributed in Canada by Irwin Publishing Inc. Distributed in the United Kingdom, Eire, Europe, Israel, and the Middle East by Phaidon Press Limited. Distributed in Japan by Yohan (Western Publications Distribution Agency).

Editor and Publisher: Paul Anbinder Typeset by Savage Type Pty Ltd, Brisbane Manufactured in Singapore by Toppan Printing Company This book was designed and produced by John Calmann and King Ltd., London Designed by Richard Foenander

Library of Congress Cataloguing in Publication Data

Gilmour, Pat.
  Ken Tyler, master printer, and the American print renaissance.

  Bibliography: p.144
  Includes index.
  1. Tyler, Kenneth E.——Criticism and interpretation. 2. Prints, American. 3. Prints——20th century——United States. I. Title.
NE539.T93G5 1986   769.92′4   85-24905
ISBN 0-933920-16-4 (alk. paper)

CONTENTS

1 David Hockney's ink drawing of Ken Tyler in the garden at Bedford Village working on *Paper pools*

INTRODUCTION

The career of Ken Tyler, who in the course of the past two decades has established himself as one of America's greatest printers, has coincided with a remarkable flowering of American printmaking. During this time, prints in general and lithographs in particular have been dramatically transformed, as major American artists have learned to make primary graphic statements in collaboration with a new breed of master printer.

In the 1940s and 1950s, the majority of American printmakers worked in etching or woodcut, and lithographs were, for the most part, black and white pictures selling for around five dollars. June Wayne, who in 1960 founded the Tamarind Lithography Workshop where Tyler studied to become a printer, has said that some of these lithographs were made so poorly she used to 'pick them up like dead mice'.[1] Today, prints are a major art form with a potential as great as painting or sculpture and one of the images Tyler produced for Frank Stella in 1984 retails at thirty thousand U.S. dollars.

plate 111

Hundreds of artists, printers and entrepreneurs have helped to make this 'print renaissance' possible, but Tyler, said to have 'Americanized print production with Detroit efficiency',[2] has enjoyed (or perhaps suffered from) particularly high visibility. In the first decade of his career as a printer, not only art journals, but magazines of general circulation such as *Life* and *Time*, broadcast his activity nationwide. The critic Robert Hughes portrayed him as a flamboyant innovator and 'vibrant impresario' supplying his 'stars' with everything from Arches cover paper to limousines and sushi fish.[3] Print specialist Judith Goldman described Tyler as 'an impetuous technological Houdini',[4] while another writer said his business sense would have stirred the admiration of the Baroque artist, Peter Paul Rubens.[5] Tyler began his work in printmaking on the assumption that 'anything is possible'[6] and his reputation for getting things done on a lavish and spectacular scale has caused commentators to compare him to Samuel Goldwyn or Cecil B. de Mille. Gemini, the firm he founded in Los Angeles in the mid-sixties, was dubbed the Metro-Goldwyn-Mayer of print workshops.

Tyler was one of eighteen master printers to pass through Tamarind during its first decade, and, in the opinion of *Life* magazine, was 'its most successful alumnus'.[7] Although he is well aware that Tamarind gave him his start and that the career he forged could not have existed without it, there were aspects of the workshop against which Tyler reacted. His experiences helped him formulate his own philosophy, a major plank of which was the belief that craftsmen working in a society based on technology and automation had to capitalize on new materials and techniques.

plate 12

Among the most important of Tyler's early influences was Josef Albers, an artist with whom he collaborated on two important Tamarind portfolios. Albers, who had been both student and master at the Bauhaus between the wars, opposed the belief that the handmade was necessarily better than the machine-made, or that a mechanical construction was anti-graphic or unable to arouse emotion. 'In this age of industrial evolution', the artist said in a statement of 1961, 'both methods have their merits'.[8] June Wayne and Clinton Adams, who together ran Tamarind, agree that Tyler was the perfect printer for Albers and that the suites *Day and night* and *Midnight and noon*

2 Sidney B. Felsen, who helped Ken Tyler form Gemini G.E.L. in 1966

3 Stanley Grinstein, who also helped Ken Tyler form Gemini G.E.L. in 1966

'moved lithography ahead'.[9] Albers, too, realized he had found an outstanding collaborator.

In 1965 Tyler set up his first workshop, Gemini Ltd., in Los Angeles. The following year he renamed the shop Gemini G.E.L. (Graphic Editions Ltd.), when he took on two partners to help develop it as a publishing house, rather than as an establishment *plates 2-3* for custom printing. At this time, Albers not only agreed to work with the new company, but donated to it, as working capital, four-fifths of the profits from his seventeen *White line squares*. This first suite to be published by Gemini G.E.L. developed an important theory about the interaction of colour and required such technical precision for its expression that Albers would have been quite unable to paint its equivalent by hand. Few people know that when Tyler tackled this most challenging and demanding work he was suffering from a back injury so severe that he had to wear a steel corset. Only seven months after setting up his first shop, he had hurt himself so seriously that he was obliged to spend almost a month in hospital. He kept this fact secret, because he was afraid that if he revealed his physical incapacity it would put his new business in jeopardy. The courage he displayed in the face of this long-standing disability makes his subsequent achievements the more remarkable.

The art world, which is quick to cast people into stereotypes and thrives on the creation of myth, continually contrasted the allegedly polished and flashy Hollywood manufacture informed by Tyler's 'industrial aesthetic' with the limited edition old-world craftsmanship of the remarkable east coast publisher, Tanya Grosman, of Universal Limited Art Editions (U.L.A.E.). One writer actually contended that, in the first eight years of its existence, Gemini was to U.L.A.E. as film director Stanley Kubrick (of *2001 — A Space Odyssey*) is to Luis Buñuel (of *The Discreet Charm of the Bourgeoisie*).[10] As Maurice Tuchman of the Los Angeles County Museum subsequently recalled, a typical viewpoint in the early days was that 'Tyler cooks with diesel fuel and Grosman cooks with schmaltz . . . one is more earthy and emotional, the other more scrubbed, clean and efficient looking'.[11]

The art world often cast its vote for what seemed most familiar. In the latter part of the 1960s, when the super-stars Jasper Johns and Robert Rauschenberg were jetting coast-to-coast making prints at both houses, Tyler's editions for them, despite *plates 26-28, 30-33,* their beauty, were frequently adversely compared with the earlier work the same *35-37, 39-40* artists had done for Tanya Grosman. Moreover, when in 1971 the Museum of Modern Art in New York honoured Gemini with the exhibition *Technics and Creativity*, the show was roundly condemned. Its curator, Riva Castleman, who had written a thoughtful essay about technological developments in printmaking, was accused by the critic Hilton Kramer in the *New York Times*[12] of promotional writing more appropriate for a bright new corporation in *Fortune* business magazine. The Jasper Johns multiple, which was part of the catalogue, was dismissed as a trivial gimmick, indicating to Kramer that the Museum had joined Gemini — a firm he castigated as a commercial press only interested in money — in the gold rush. About the most complimentary assessment of the West Coast prints at this time was that they were elegant, sleek, chic and flawless, although even the latter implied a pejorative to those who found fingerprints in the margin 'more human'. Others claimed that the images issued by Gemini were antiseptic, depersonalized and reproductive, and, in the tradition of east coast snobbism (detected in those who live on the 'right' side of the Hudson River by those who don't), much was derogatively made of 'the Los Angeles fetish finish'.

Nevertheless, as time went on many of Tyler's prints, including those he had helped the so-called U.L.A.E. artists to make, were recognized as the masterpieces they had always been and as 'monuments in the history of American graphic art'.[13] When the Pratt Graphics Center asked curators and dealers to survey the quarter century since 1956 and to nominate the twenty-five best American prints made in the period, U.L.A.E. and Gemini outdid all other publishers, achieving equal honours with four prints each. The experts agreed that U.L.A.E.'s finest contributions during the period had been Robert Motherwell's *Gauloises bleues* (1968), James Rosenquist's *Off the continental divide* (1973/4), Helen Frankenthaler's *East and beyond* (1973) and Jasper Johns' *Decoy I* (1971) — the latter an offset print that Tanya Grosman would not have countenanced when she began publishing. The most successful prints from Gemini were judged to be Albers' *White line square XIII* (1966), Roy Lichtenstein's *Cathedral #3* (1969), Robert Rauschenberg's *Booster* (1967) and Frank Stella's *Star of Persia I* (1967). Although the cut-off date for their selection was 1981, the experts were not daring enough to name more than one print after 1975; with the benefit of

plate 42
plate 4

4 Frank Stella: *Star of Persia I*, 1967, 26 x 31 in (66.0 x 78.7 cm), lithograph, edition 92

hindsight, however, they decided that Gemini's best graphic works (all of which Tyler not only published but helped to print) had been created earlier than those they considered the cream from the famous east coast publisher.

Although one of Gemini's printers, Timothy Isham, felt that Tyler's dynamic personality dominated the west coast shop and that 'everything pretty much depended on his personal wizardry',[14] in 1973 Tyler decided to leave his two partners and to start afresh on his own. Gemini had grown to such a size that he had trouble remembering the names of all the staff and he felt the 'showbiz' side of things was beginning to have a bad effect on him. He wanted to return to a smaller operation because, after the economic downturn occasioned by the oil crisis, print publishing was changing, together with his own ideas about it. Raising the money he needed by selling his printer's proofs, together with preparatory works and drawings that grateful artists had dedicated to him,[15] to the Australian National Gallery in Canberra, Tyler founded a new workshop in Bedford Village, some thirty-five miles north of New York City. Once again Josef Albers christened the venture, this time with *Gray instrumentation*, a   plate 25 screenprinted suite of exquisite subtlety.

While this suite and other Bedford Village prints manifest the familiar clarity and precision or 'Tyler look', the range of Tyler's work in the east has been enormously expanded by his fascination for handmade paper. This interest developed following a project the printer undertook with Robert Rauschenberg in France in 1973. The 'very American cross'[16] he subsequently cooked up in Bedford Village, between the most advanced and the oldest print technologies, once again displayed outstanding invention and energy.

Tyler's name crops up in almost any discussion about American printmaking; it excites every reaction from praise to blame and every emotion from admiration to envy. Few can disregard his impact on recent graphic art. Although many can claim to have assisted in the remarkable revaluation of printmaking that has taken place over the past two decades, Tyler's contribution has been of particular brilliance and the artists with whom he has worked recognize that they have participated in a new intensity of collaboration.

Among the most dramatic items to emerge from Tyler's east coast shop are works like David Hockney's *Paper pools* and the equally beautiful abstract images made by   plates 70-73 other artists lured by the printer to manipulate the raw materials of papermaking at the wet stage, so as virtually to paint or sculpt with pulp. In a book about his experiences, Hockney said that he found working with someone of Tyler's energy 'very thrilling . . . With Ken Tyler, nothing was impossible. If I said could we, he said, yes, yes, it can be done'.[17]

The work Tyler accomplished with the painter Frank Stella represents perhaps the high point of his career. Nearly three years of effort went into a series of black and white *Swan engravings* and the many varied *Circuit* images, for which Tyler created   plates 105-108, 111 extraordinary large-scale multicoloured papers. These complex mixed-media images, with their remarkable awareness of surface texture, have been hailed as virtuoso prints that transcend mere virtuosity. In their integrity and independence they win for graphic art a status comparable to that of painting. 'I'm lucky', said Stella in an interview in 1983, 'I believe the printers I've worked with are the very best. I know Ken thinks he's great, and he is! He loves the challenge'.[18]

For Helen Frankenthaler and Robert Motherwell, Tyler has demonstrated his capacity to serve the complete spectrum of aesthetic sensibilities, since neither artist is exactly suited to an 'industrial aesthetic'. Indeed, abstract artists whose work is based on gesture have the greatest difficulties in coming to terms with editioned art and in trying to bridge the gap between being an artist and a printmaker — as critic Jules Langsner put it, 'the irreconcilable conflict between the unique attributes of the work of art and the uniform reproductive processes of the machine'.[19] Yet in September 1984, at the opening of a new building at the Walker Art Center in Minneapolis, plate 85 with a study facility devoted to Tyler's work, Robert Motherwell affirmed that the Sunday afternoons he regularly spends with the printer have been among the happiest of his life. Tyler, he told the audience at the dedication, was the greatest technical genius in America, companionable and understanding, 'an artistic Don Juan' who had seduced him with the miracle of printmaking.[20]

THE BACKGROUND TO TYLER'S CAREER AND THE 'PRINT RENAISSANCE'

LITHOGRAPHY IN AMERICA

Although many different forms of printmaking were beginning to emerge in the United States in the 1950s, the so-called print renaissance, which is usually dated from 1960, centred mainly on the lithographic process. The movement was not only confined to America, for while Tamarind and U.L.A.E. were starting up in the United States, a similar development was taking place in England. The French tradition of printing for artists did not exist there either and Stanley Jones, who had been trained in Paris, set up a pilot lithography workshop in St. Ives in 1958 and a little later opened a specialized studio in London for the Curwen Press.[1]

plate 5

5 Stanley Jones, master printer of Curwen Studio, London (pulling a proof of a lithograph by Ceri Richards in 1965)

Lithography (a word derived from the Greek words for 'stone' and 'writing') was invented at the end of the eighteenth century by a Bavarian called Alois Senefelder who was looking for a cheap way of duplicating his plays. Senefelder found it was possible to print both texts and pictures from an image made in a greasy substance on a slab of fine limestone quarried near his home. The revolutionary aspect of his process was that, unlike the existing relief and intaglio techniques which employed cut wood or engraved metal, it required no force, nor did the image have to be translated into a codified system of lines and dots. The method consisted quite simply of drawing on the flat grained surface of the stone and then treating the image chemically to prepare it for printing. When the stone was sponged with water, the undrawn areas on its surface repelled the oily ink applied by roller, whereas the grease of the artist's drawing, which filled the stone's other pores, had an affinity for the ink and accepted it for transfer to paper.

Lithography thus joined relief and intaglio printing as one of the nineteenth century's three main methods for making graphic art. It fulfilled a largely reproductive function until the middle of the century, when the concept of the 'original print' began to take shape. This term was increasingly used to differentiate prints for which the artist had personally crafted the printing matrix in order to capitalize on the technique's expressive qualities. Although French artists such as Géricault, Manet, Fantin-Latour and Redon made black and white lithographs as an original means of expression, the dominant form of the process, particularly in America, was the chromolithograph — a colour print made by craftsmen carrying out other artists' designs. It was only in the late 1880s that original colour lithography emerged in France, although even then it was associated with commercial posters.[2]

The first lithographic press in America was established in 1819. Reproductive lithography took root so successfully, however, that by 1890 there were more than seven hundred printing establishments employing eight thousand people for a total yearly production valued at twenty million dollars.[3] From this point onward, commercial lithography began to develop as a much swifter rotary process. Cumbersome limestone slabs, the larger examples of which could weigh several hundred pounds, were dispensed with in favour of metal plates which could be curved onto a cylinder. The direct press, where the paper received the image straight from the drawn stone or metal substitutes, gave way to a more mechanical system based on the offset principle, in which a continuous rubber blanket transferred the image from the plate to the sheet of paper.

In America, where the technique was probably doubly despised because of its commercial connection with cheap colour reproductions, lithography was used under the auspices of the Federal Art Project during the Depression for narrative or social realist prints dealing with the American scene. These prints were produced in large and inexpensive editions, thereby reinforcing their modest nineteenth-century associations and fulfilling the democratic ideal of putting art within the reach of all. A few professional printers still ministered to lithographic artists' needs, but the prevailing aesthetic required only simple and predictable crayon work, the printing of which was not particularly demanding. Even so, by 1940 the art historian H. W. Janson noted a dearth of fine art lithographic craftsmen and warned that the survival of lithography could be at stake.[4] The outbreak of the second world war did not improve the situation.

By this time those American artists who had fallen in love with the silken sensitivity of the stone — so sensuously responsive that early draftsmen were warned to control their dandruff and to be careful that their sneezes did not affect the image on its surface — found themselves flying in the face of technological progress and dedicated to an anachronism. What was worse, the stone from Senefelder's incomparable Bavarian quarry was in short supply and, as commercial lithographers switched to offset, their stones were dumped. During the 1960s, for example, Tyler rescued about one hundred stones from a batch that an Ohio firm was giving to the construction company building the Newport-Cincinnati freeway, and at the time he announced his willingness to fly anywhere in America to rescue more.[5]

When *Time* wrote up the Los Angeles Tamarind Lithography Workshop in 1964 as 'a messianic attempt to revive the making of graphic art from stone', it also spoke of lithography as being 'more direct and spontaneous than other graphic arts. No chiseling, no carving or etching is required . . . the artist just draws . . .'[6] It was just this autographic quality — the fact that the nuance of any mark recorded could be transferred to the printed page — that 'enchanted' Tyler[7] and made the process so suitable for the 1950s aesthetic based on gesture. However, as the writer Michael Crichton decided after speaking at some length to the printer, this was not the whole story:

> The printmaking process is very far from the life of a solitary painter, alone with his brushes, his canvas and his thoughts. For a painter, lithography demands not only a whole range of new techniques — on a stone, for example, everything must be drawn backwards and in only one colour at a time — but an entirely different method of working. Printmaking is a collaborative process, an interaction . . .[8]

To complicate matters, the density of any mark depends not on the blackness of the tusche, or lithographic drawing medium (which comes in sticks of different hardness or washes of varying fluidity coloured simply to make them visible), but on the amount of grease deposited into the stone's receptive surface. Finally, the delay between making the mark on stone and receiving the proof of what has been drawn may be protracted. The much vaunted spontaneity that the technique can theoretically offer a painter is therefore relative, although the process does aspire to more immediacy than most other branches of printmaking.

While a woodcut may be simply printed by manual pressure or the rubbing of the back of an impression with a spoon, the intricacy of both the chemical and mechanical procedures of lithography and the necessity for a press have usually meant that artists working with the process needed expert assistance. In France, where the colour lithographic revolution of the 1890s spread widely among avant-garde painters, a body of printers specializing in such work grew up and, because of the concentration of artists in Paris, survived into the twentieth century. When the 1950s style based on painterly gesture emerged, French artisans were able to serve the artist with appropriate lithographic washes. Since these printers did not readily share their trade secrets, American printers did not have access to their skills until Tamarind began training its printers, although prior to this there were pockets of informed activity.

The conversion of an artist's lithographic drawing into printer's ink is problematic, particularly when fugitive washes are at stake. The preparation of the stone entails a process somewhat confusingly known as 'the etch', which has no connection with the same term used in intaglio printing, but instead fixes and stabilizes the artist's greasy drawing. There is great subtlety in the way the printer preserves and develops the image latent in the grease and this, together with the skill subsequently used to roll it up with ink, gives the lithograph its distinctive quality. Because of the number of variables which can adversely affect the outcome, Tyler has usually taken upon himself the responsibility for etching the lithographs made in his shops. The humidity and temperature of studio or workshop, the frailty or strength of the artist's drawing, the length of time a stone has been stored, the exact volume and strength of the acidified gum arabic (which the printer often tests by tasting) — all of these factors amount to a microclimate which the printer must know intimately in order to achieve the best results. As Tyler told Michael Crichton:

> Some people are gifted. It's like being able to raise plants. Some people are heavy-handed, some sensitive like a surgeon . . . I have to say, most people are butchers. They have little regard for subtleties, which their eyes don't even pick up . . . I'm always frightened to death when I do something to a stone and I'm terribly relieved when I see the image developing in the way I remembered it. There's no substitution for this — I think you always have to be frightened.[9]

6 Picasso: *Pigeon on a grey background*, 1947, 17¼ x 10¼ in (43.8 x 26.0 cm), lithograph, edition 50

Ben Berns, a printer who worked for Tanya Grosman, has explained the relative safety of processing a crayon lithograph, compared to the risks involved in developing a wash: '*Your stone is basically alive* and *each stone is different* in the way it reacts to the treatment of the printer. Some stones are very stable, others are not.'[10]

The process becomes even more difficult when stones are printed, chemically 'closed', then put away and later opened again for further printing; printers have always been reluctant to provide such time-consuming services unless the status of the artist seemed likely to ensure them an adequate return for their trouble. This was the case with the most famous Ecole de Paris artists, whose prints enjoyed a huge popularity in the United States after the war. Some of the colour lithographs from Europe gave renewed ethical fervour to the debate over definitions of originality, since they were largely reproductive prints, made after gouaches by craftsmen whose exact role was undeclared.

The personal involvement of Picasso, however, was to transform the process. As Tyler told a discussion group he chaired in 1975, Picasso virtually 'reinvented the art of lithography for us. I wouldn't be a printmaker today without seeing his prints'.[11] One of Picasso's motivations for taking up lithography again after the war was the fact that the Paris workshop of the printer Mourlot was heated, whereas his own studio was not!

In the 1930s Picasso had worked with Roger Lacourière to expand the possibilities for etching — now, in the 1940s and 1950s, he was to do the same for lithography. Fascinated, the artist would work long hours in Mourlot's atelier until every facet of the technique became second nature to him, and 'he compelled a brilliant but traditionally intransigent group of master craftsmen to find technical solutions outside routine and customary practice'.[12] Mourlot himself has recorded that merely to tell Picasso that there was a rule was to ensure that he broke it and his pressman 'often cursed his lithographic oddities'.[13] Tyler was amazed by the innovatory bravado with which, plate 6 in 1947, Picasso had sketched a pigeon using gouache as a negative form or resist over a lithographic wash on transfer paper. Since he felt lithography in America was hampered by rules and restrictions, Tyler was enormously influenced by such work and delighted in the anti-academic example it set.

THE IMPLICATIONS OF CHANGING STYLES FOR GRAPHIC ART

Between 1920 and 1960, the pendulum swung many times in the world at large between two basic aesthetic stances — the individualistic and the mechanistic. Since very diverse ideologies can be accommodated between the handcrafted 'original print', personalized by marginal fingerprints, and the standardized multiple from the machine shop, each stylistic fluctuation has had implications for graphic art and for the public's perception of the so-called industrial aesthetic Tyler was to adopt in 1965.

Between the wars, European Constructivism, with its acceptance of the machine, had been founded on faith in rationality and the possibility of building a perfect world. Early Constructivists expressed interest in a systematic means of expression that would be universally comprehensible; some aspects of this philosophy were viewed as particularly American. At the Bauhaus, where Walter Gropius dreamed of a new unity between art and technology, Oscar Schlemmer, one of the school's teachers, noted how initial expressionist leanings had given way to 'the American spirit, progress, the marvels of technology and invention, the urban environment'.[1] Louis Lozowick, the American Precisionist invited to write one of the famous Bauhaus books, said in an article on 'The Americanization of Art': 'The dominant trend in America of today is towards an industrialization and standardization which require precise adjustment of structure to function . . . [and] . . . which foster in man a spirit of objectivity excluding all emotional aberration . . .'[2]

Other American Precisionists (who were also known as Immaculates, or Sterilists) included Charles Sheeler and the photographer Paul Strand, both of whom delighted in the industrial scene as subject matter.

As Concrete Art developed out of Constructivism during the 1930s, individualism, sentimentality, lyricism, symbolism and impressionist rendering were rejected in favour of works composed of plastic elements.[3] These works had no meaning outside themselves, but used industrial materials with impersonal clarity. Since they were premeditated, made without reliance on a personal 'handwriting', and conceived in advance of execution, they made possible collective production and the increased use of assistants. The camera, later to be outlawed from 'original' printmaking as a mechanical device, was at this time still adopted as one tool among many new options available for use by artists.

The use of the word 'mechanical' itself has an interesting history, for the term has usually had pejorative connotations. From the fifteenth century on, it denoted the main range of non-agricultural productive work and gradually came to refer to any routine unthinking activity to which social prejudice attached. By extension, and when applied to forces in the universe, 'mechanical' later assumed materialist — as opposed to spiritual or idealist — implications.[4]

Even before the war, Surrealism, with its irrationality, its interest in the subconscious mind and its sly, mechanically interpreted eroticism, helped undermine the century's optimistic spirit. In the wake of Hiroshima, much of humanity's confidence in technological progress was shaken. Throughout the 1940s and 1950s, individualized gesture and psychic automatism were dominant again, while the prevailing view of the creative process, best characterized in H. W. Janson's *History of Art*, was one in which conception and execution could not be separated, because the artist 'never quite knows what he is making until he has actually made it' and 'is not sure what he is looking for until he has found it'.[5]

When organic abstraction emerged after the second world war, the movement was world-wide. The European equivalent of Abstract Expressionism, the style which brought international recognition to American painting, was known as 'Tachism' (from the French word for stain). The dealer Denise René, who was committed to a group of artists working in a form of geometric abstraction stemming from Constructivism, has given an amusing if understandably prejudiced account of how, just as the great Constructivists of an earlier generation had been submerged by Surrealism, so the 'tachist bomb' now exploded, almost obliterating her own protégés. There was a flood tide 'of lyric abstraction, Action painting, Abstract Expressionism and Convulsive art; there were the nuagistes (cloud makers) and the Matter School'.[6] The new style swept the market and miles of 'incessant splodgings' took over the international Documenta exhibition in Kassel in 1960. 'We were like a political minority in exile', Denise René later wrote of those she represented, 'the Fidel Castros of Constructivism, looking for a landing place. Someone suggested a mock exhibition of machine-made tachist canvases as a demonstration of the public herd instinct'.[7] And Jean Tinguely, as if in response, although with rather more poetic intentions, presented his amusing Meta-matic machines for mass-producing abstract art.

By this time, as communist and capitalist societies ranged themselves against one another, the industrial aesthetic, which before the war had seemed so American, now typified mechanized standardization and the collectivist principle. The expressionist and the intuitively 'human', on the other hand, came to represent the faith in the ultimate liberty of the individual espoused by the western democracies.

To a certain extent, even if photomechanical procedures are forbidden, any printed edition utilizing a press draws on technology and is an industrial product. This fact, together with the commercial implications of printmaking, almost certainly prejudiced the Abstract Expressionist generation of American artists against it. Equally, although the lithographic process invited spontaneous gesture and coincided so completely with the Expressionists' notions about originality in printmaking, it failed during their 'heroic' early period to arouse their interest. This was due, perhaps, to the need the process presented for collaborative technical resolution. First generation Abstract Expressionists like Jackson Pollock, Willem de Kooning and Robert Motherwell confined their printmaking to a rather limited amount of work at S. W. Hayter's co-operative intaglio workshop. Even so, it has been suggested that a short exposure to the automatism which Hayter demonstrated in his use of the engraving tool on metal helped liberate Pollock, facilitating his break-through to the characteristic form of all-over abstraction for which he became world-famous.[8]

Hayter was an Englishman who opened his first workshop in Paris in 1927. The shop, which was called Atelier 17, was dedicated to experimentation in intaglio printmaking, a process in which the image is created either by engraving a line directly into the metal plate or by incising it indirectly by etching it with acid. Hayter captivated nearly every important artist of his generation by his openness, his enthusiasm, his astute intelligence and his refreshing unpretentiousness. During the second world war, at a time 'when you couldn't give a modern print away in America',[9] Hayter transferred his workshop to New York, where it continued to attract famous exiled European artists and new American recruits.

Robert Motherwell has described Hayter's atelier as 'a beehive of professional activity, of optimism, of accomplishment, of sheer human decency, of the will to continue'.[10] For American modernists weaned on realism and social protest, the ambience Hayter provided was extremely sympathetic, although, as Motherwell went on to note, the American print world at the time was one in which 'there were artists and "printmakers" and very rarely did the lines cross'. The problem was (and, to a certain extent, still is) that the 'artists' looked with disdain on the technical 'cookery' in which specialized printmakers allegedly indulged. The painter Franz Kline apparently also felt that graphic art was so inferior as a form of expression, and so inextricably identified with craft, that he advised a young artist not to associate himself with it if he wanted to 'make it' in New York.[11]

In one respect, the American collaborative workshop, as it developed after June Wayne's efforts at Tamarind, helped break down the reservations artists had that the techniques of printmaking might inhibit their image-making. The close collaboration with a professional printer that June Wayne advocated distanced artists from the technicalities some of them considered dangerous. On the other hand, there was a certain theoretical force in Hayter's submission that only if the artist carried out every part of the process, including the printing, would the truly 'original print' — at which everyone was then aiming — be produced.

In fact Hayter, a warm and generous character who said anyone who believed in art for art's sake should try talk for talking's sake, differentiated no fewer than five degrees of originality in printmaking.[12] A work, he said, could only be of major significance if the technique itself contributed to the transposition of the idea. This, he felt, was far more likely to occur in the almost sculptural complexities of intaglio than in lithography, since to him a lithograph rarely seemed to be more than a multiplied drawing. During the 1950s and early 1960s, Hayter's techniques for simultaneous colour printing by the control of ink viscosities penetrated to every corner of the globe, visually dominating one print biennale after another.

It was almost twenty years after his brief spell of printmaking in Hayter's workshop that Robert Motherwell eventually made lithographs, first with U.L.A.E., then with the ex-Tamarind printer, Irwin Hollander. The typical form of expression, both for Motherwell and for other Abstract Expressionists like de Kooning, was the gestural mark of a single colour which allowed the printer to answer the artists' need for immediacy by giving them 'a fast serve'.[13]

Hayter's advocacy of complete control found few disciples among painters unwilling to devote time to the requisite craft apprenticeship. His conceptual analysis, however, raised interesting questions about the aesthetic element contributed by platemaking or printing during a collaboration and may well have exacerbated the rift between 'artists' and 'printmakers'. Nevertheless, the now widely accepted idea that a print should capitalize on essentially graphic qualities rather than imitate other media owes its acceptance largely to the force of Hayter's arguments.

In the late 1950s, however, at the peak of Hayter's influence, the pendulum swung again and the theory and practice of Abstract Expressionism was undermined by a two-pronged attack from quite different directions, one of which, with its roots in Constructivism, was 'hard-edge' painting. This development, as the art historian George Heard Hamilton put it, was defined less by its crisp edges 'than by the fact that such works are planned in advance of their execution' and were thus 'susceptible to intellectual control rather than of the free play of instinctual responses . . .' In the other movement, which was to be known as Pop Art, painters attempted to erode the barriers between art and life by introducing real and often disreputable non-art objects into their work. As this strategy developed, photographs, which had already been converted into print by the mass communications media, were incorporated once again into printmaking. Since even their painted canvases drew on printed sources, Pop artists became particularly adept at thinking graphically. The artist and critic John Loring went so far as to say that Pop artists were 'graphic artists of great genius who also painted'.[14] This, together with the suitability of the hard-edge style to industrial techniques, fostered a climate hospitable to forms of printmaking far removed from the expressionist ethos.

Gradually, as the balance of power shifted from Paris to New York and Abstract Expressionist paintings became very large and expensive, the more modest scale and price of prints began to supply the lower end of a growing market. The booming economy revived a spirit of optimism in the art world and commerce was no longer quite such a dirty word. As the growing middle class enjoyed increased leisure and more disposable income, museums began to cater for a wider public rather than for a tiny cultural élite; this also helped give a larger financial basis to the growing print market.

In a little over a decade, graphic art was transformed. From a despised activity in which only an occasional painter indulged, it became so popular that the artist who did not make prints became an exception. As an artist friend told the art editor Thomas Hess:

> In the fifties when you saw a friend on the Long Island Railroad on an early Wednesday morning, you knew he was going to town to see his shrink. Nowadays, you know he's on his way to work with his lithographer.[15]

It was on the crest of this wave that Tyler went into business.

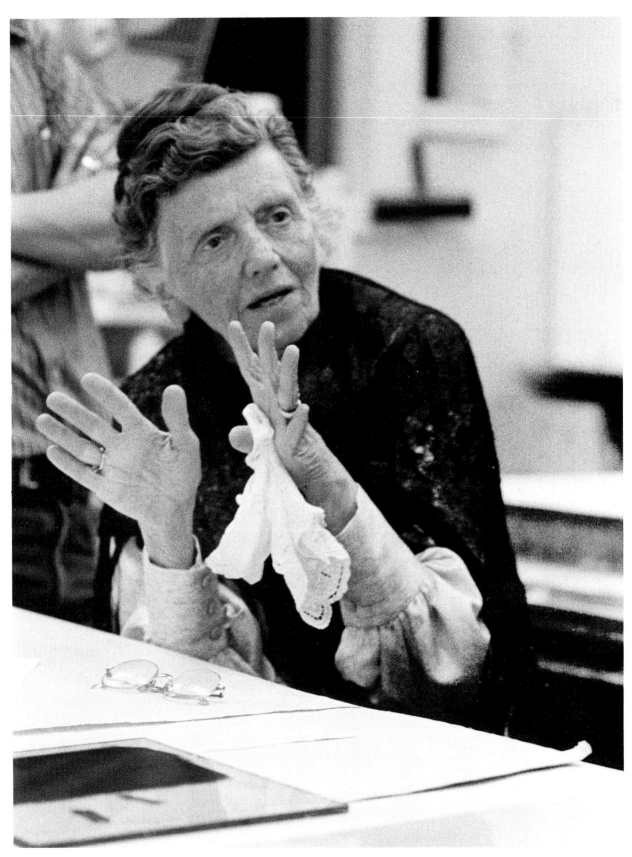

7 Tatyana Grosman at Universal Limited Art Editions, West Islip, in 1977

TWO LITHOGRAPHIC INSTITUTIONS

UNIVERSAL LIMITED ART EDITIONS

Although Tyler had trained at Tamarind, he also looked with admiration at the output from Universal Limited Art Editions which had begun to excite public enthusiasm a few years before he went into business. Both these lithographic institutions had an extremely important influence on the formation of his philosophy and both came to fruition in the years 1959/60.

plate 7 Tanya Grosman of U.L.A.E., whose print activity stemmed from an intense love of books, was the daughter of a Russian newspaper publisher in the Ural town of Ekaterinburg, where the Czar was executed during the revolution. Displaced by political events, she became a student at the Dresden Academy of Applied Arts and met and later married the Jewish artist, Maurice Grosman. After their wedding the Grosmans moved to Paris, but, as Hitler overran Europe and his master plan for the Jews became evident, they moved on again, leaving the French capital two days before it fell. After a period of terrifying and interminable delays, they walked across the Pyrenees to Spain, eventually escaping to the United States and safety; these wartime adventures were to become part of Tanya Grosman's myth. When Barnett Newman produced his famous *XVIII cantos* at her workshop, succumbing to the combination of charm and implacable persistence with which she persuaded the most famous artists to give prints a try, he apologized to another publisher with whom he had refused to work. 'If a woman has enough persistence to walk across the Pyrenees to escape from the Germans, you know she is going to get you in the end'.[1]

Tanya Grosman's first artist — Larry Rivers — writing after her death in 1982, referred to her life as 'a grand and satisfying fairy tale'.[2] Certainly the U.L.A.E. mystique was powerfully reinforced by the fact that its founder interpreted her own existence in terms of a series of minor miracles. When she first turned to publishing in the mid-fifties after her husband suffered a heart attack, the summer house at West Islip, New York, which eventually became the U.L.A.E. workshop, 'fell from heaven' through a chance encounter with a Dominican priest.[3] Then, after the influential American curators, W. S. Lieberman and Carl Zigrosser, advised her to produce original prints rather than the high quality screenprinted reproductions on which she first embarked, she decided she wanted an artist 'to work with his hand on a surface'.[4] Presto! She happened upon two old lithographic stones in her garden path. Something told her such stones might be used to make the kind of de luxe books she had just been reading about[5] — books that united the work of poets and painters. When she went to discuss the possibility with her artist friend Rivers, she found the poet Frank O'Hara, whom someone else had recommended to her, actually visiting Rivers that day. And so, in 1957, the idea for her first 'original' publication, *Stones*, was born. It comes as no surprise to learn that a neighbour just happened to have a second-hand lithography press, which Tanya Grosman bought for the give-away price of fifteen dollars.

U.L.A.E.'s prints were produced — first in Mrs Grosman's dining-room and later in her garage — with a slow deliberation that took no account of the maxim that 'time is money'. The firm's business records, kept by the poet Tony Towle, were, according to Larry Rivers, 'terrible'. Although Tanya Grosman had set up her business ostensibly to support herself and her sick husband, and in the early days experienced 'anxiety about getting a print to market',[6] it was the opinion of the supportive Lieberman, who found subscribers to help her, that her commercial operation, 'if indeed there is one', was incidental.[7] However, the Art Institute of Chicago paid 1.2 million dollars for 542 prints Mrs Grosman had published and when she died in 1982 Bill Goldston, her master printer and successor, found this sum useful for settling U.L.A.E.'s debts. Today these prints reside in Chicago, together with Mrs Grosman's gift of 4,200 working proofs. Goldston says he learned everything he knows about art and life from U.L.A.E.'s founder, and that he has accepted her value system in its entirety: 'You can't really have any financial concerns in making art'.[8]

Nor could art, in Tanya Grosman's opinion, be rushed, although artists sometimes found her extravagance with time tedious. James Rosenquist, who nevertheless made some of his finest lithographs at U.L.A.E., felt that waiting a year to see a proof was 'like picking up a stale sandwich and having to take another bite out of it'.[9] Jasper Johns also commented that by the time he saw the results of one action, he had often decided on something else,[10] and he described the whole printmaking operation as rather like 'a long distance call through an overseas operator'.[11]

The leisurely West Islip day was, however, part of Tanya Grosman's essential style and the legendary lunches — 'Mom's kitchen from Dostoyevsky's *Notes from the Underground*'[12] as Rivers described them — became a central event, at which the maternal Tanya, her artists, her printers, and the increasing flow of curatorial visitors sat down at the communal table.

Although she was reputedly gentle and subscribed to the romantic view of 'the artist as a superior individual and art as the creation of genius',[13] Tanya Grosman could wield an iron fist in her velvet glove when it came to aesthetic matters. For example, she once told Motherwell that he must clean his own margins as nobody else could properly do that for him,[14] while Rivers found that, as time went on, she 'began editing like an impresario who thinks he knows better than the artist what is good and how to bring that out'.[15] Rivers had other differences with Mrs Grosman and for four years engaged with her in a battle of wills over a sculptural multiple he wanted to make of his girlfriend. The battle eventually resulted in compromise.

Since Tanya Grosman's own view on lithography had been influenced when she began publishing by curatorial thinking based on the 'originality' definitions, that concept defined the parameters of her aesthetic approach. Until Bill Goldston came aboard and persuaded her differently, she felt that offset prints could not be art. She refused to publish Ellsworth Kelly and told him his work was 'a denial of everything that lithography is'.[16] Her sensibility about what she did encompass was such, however, that the artists accepted her judgement, looked to her for approval and strove 'to go beyond themselves'.[17] In the most poetic of appreciations, Motherwell wrote of her workshop as a place 'where it is simply assumed, as seldom elsewhere nowadays, that the world of the spirit exists as concretely as lemon yellow or woman's hair but transcends everyday life'.[18] He little guessed that because he went, shortly afterwards, to work with Tyler at Gemini, Tanya Grosman 'as a kind of punishment'[19] would never ask him back to U.L.A.E. For although in some reports she sounded philosophically sanguine about 'her' artists working elsewhere and said she welcomed the ideas they brought back as she could learn from them,[20] she was in fact fiercely possessive. When Irwin Hollander began working with Jim Dine, she threatened legal action, 'screamed and went crazy',[21] and Hollander, rather than embarrass the artist by conflict, backed down.

Tanya Grosman's business attitudes were obviously sympathetic to the growing need artists felt in the 1960s to stress other values in the face of art's increasingly rapacious escalation as a capitalist commodity. Equally, her rather naive technical approach, which entailed denying all knowledge of production matters and claiming technique was unimportant (while often specifying, nevertheless, exactly how things were to be done), was attractive to artists who were primarily painters or sculptors and who wanted to differentiate their graphic art from that produced by 'printmakers' overly concerned with craft. Both these attitudes coincided with the critical and curatorial ideologies that were dominant when Tanya Grosman began work. Many commentators have explained Mrs Grosman's intuitive feeling for the possibilities of lithography in terms of her Parisian experience. In fact, she herself categorically denied any knowledge of the process prior to founding U.L.A.E. and said she had only a knowledge of art and artists.[22] Technical matters were for the printer.

The first among the many printers employed at U.L.A.E. was Robert Blackburn, who since 1949 had run a co-operative workshop in New York which was based on Hayter's Atelier 17 model but which practised lithography. Tyler still remembers how impressed he was when he saw Johns' *Coat hanger*. Although these were technically primitive days, he thinks Blackburn was an exceptional printer and was very impressed by the work he saw coming from Tanya Grosman's workshop. When he printed U.L.A.E.'s first publication, Blackburn had to contend with stones that had not only done interim service as a pathway, but were badly grained into the bargain. Moreover, Tanya Grosman insisted that their chipped and irregular perimeters should be inked and embedded into the paper, a characteristic Blackburn felt she had borrowed from intaglio printing. In fact, this approach to the lithograph is closer to that of the German Expressionist group, *Die Brücke*,[23] and if any European stimuli informed Tanya Grosman's attitude to lithography, they seem just as likely to have come from Dresden as from Paris. Certainly the device she insisted upon served as a rather naive way of informing people that they were looking at an original print made by hand and not at a mass-produced artefact. Although Mrs Grosman told a researcher that the artist's wishes were paramount and that she directed the printer 'to do nothing which would meddle or interfere with the artist's work',[24] the perimeter that surrounded each image in *Stones* stemmed from her rather than from Larry Rivers. Even Blackburn resisted the publisher's wishes because of the danger that he might break the rare and expensive stones. It thus becomes a classic example of the way technique and aesthetic are actually imposed, even by publishers who say it is their policy not to interfere, and it illuminates the collaborative nature of any graphic work.

As a matter of fact it was also a strategy of German Expressionists like Erich Heckel to continue printing from broken stones. Just such a disaster, however, finally made Blackburn return to his own workshop when a stone drawn by Rauschenberg, the print from which was appropriately entitled *Accident*, broke in the press. Zigmunds Priede, who succeeded Blackburn as U.L.A.E.'s printer, managed to get an edition from the diagonally riven stone complete with its cluster of broken chips. Although *Accident* is a marvellous image that with its acceptance of chance perfectly encapsulates Rauschenberg's existential approach, it is not without irony that this cavalier treatment of the rarest ingredient of hand lithography won the fifth international graphic biennale in Ljubljana in 1963, securing a major prize for the artist a year before he won the grand prize for painting in Venice.

In her obituary of Tanya Grosman, Riva Castleman suggested that her personality had so overshadowed her workshop that 'the contribution of her staff easily went unrecognized'.[25] Even had this not been the case, neither she nor Blackburn would have stressed the printer's contribution, since both were committed to 'the near sanctity of the artist's work'. In retrospect, the input of the U.L.A.E. printers must have been crucial, but Blackburn tells a story, fascinating for the attitudes it reveals, of how, at a time when she was so hard up that paying him meant not paying the telephone bill, Tanya Grosman would spend money she did not have to provide scallops for 'her artists'. After everybody had gone, Blackburn told a researcher, 'she would go and make a little bowl of soup for herself . . . And she would also try to include me, but I was always second to the artist'.[26]

Blackburn left, after the breaking of the stone, feeling he was 'losing touch' with himself. Priede, who claimed to have trained himself by 'trial and error', did not stay either. He found suppressing his own creativity so frustrating that he gave up printing.[27] The turnover of printers in U.L.A.E.'s early years was very high, for Mrs

plate 8

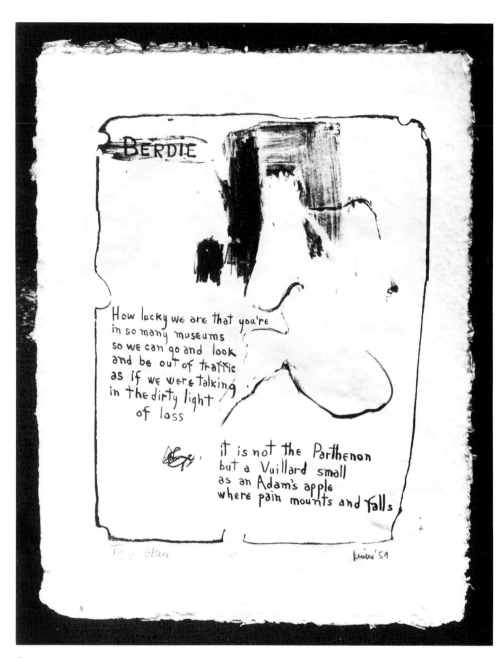

8 Larry Rivers and Frank O'Hara: page 5 *Berdie* from the portfolio *Stones*, 1957-1959, 18¾ x 23½ in (47.6 x 59.7 cm), lithograph, edition 25

Grosman was extremely demanding. 'If you couldn't have walked through the Pyrenees with Tanya', said Goldston, 'you couldn't have been a printer here!'.[28]

Another of Tanya Grosman's precepts was that the edition should be determined by what the printer, who at all costs had to avoid becoming 'mechanical', could manage to print in a day. Ben Berns, an experienced European printer who had been simultaneously invited to work at U.L.A.E. and to take over Ken Tyler's job at Tamarind, selected the former because he felt that Tamarind worked with too many artists. After years of cranking out large editions in France, he was attracted to U.L.A.E.'s very different philosophy.[29]

Although Tanya Grosman's beliefs about leisurely pace undoubtedly influenced her method of working, it also seems likely that this method was in part an answer to the difficulty of paying her printers to commute on a day-to-day basis and of maintaining quality while opening and closing stones that had once been inked. Certainly the tiny and sometimes bizarre sizes of the U.L.A.E. editions and the difference between impressions, while usefully reinforcing notions of 'originality', would not have helped in balancing the books, and, in fact, suggest a high level of wastage in order to maintain quality control.

The small editions were also affected by Tanya Grosman's sensitivity to the materials she used and by her obsession with exotic papers, of which she could sometimes obtain only a few sheets. This fascination led her to print *Stones*, her very first portfolio, on a difficult linen rag paper for which Douglass Howell was able to make a few sheets at a time 'only if it wasn't raining';[30] the portfolio cover came from blue jeans, the uniform of its creators. Jasper Johns' first famous *0–9* portfolio was delayed three years — partly, one suspects, because of the complexities the artist introduced into its printing[31] and partly by a wait for the appropriate paper. Thirteen years later, the portfolio was still causing Tanya Grosman to marvel at the different character the choice of paper could lend images from the same stone: 'First the zero, very classic in black ink on off-white paper, and then printed in gray on the unbleached paper — very mysterious and moody — and then once again, very luminously printed in yellow on pure white, like sunshine'.[32] For one print by Claes Oldenburg she tried twenty different substrates before settling for a Balinese toilet paper. Citing this example, Larry Rivers wondered whether the publisher placed rather too much emphasis on paper and rhetorically asked an interviewer: 'Can quality paper make quality prints? Thomas Hess, who loved the irreverence of Bill de Kooning painting on pages from a telephone book, thought her quality paper idea a hackneyed one and pompous'.[33]

Nevertheless, Tanya Grosman opened many American eyes — Tyler's included — to the contribution made to aesthetic quality by the basic materials of graphic art.

Without doubt, her greatest claim to fame will rest on her relentless will and the fact that, with the inevitability of pilgrims' lips eroding St. Peter's toe, she was able to persuade the greatest American artists of the day to rethink their attitudes to prints. By gaining the backing of influential curators and by the mystique she created with her old-world charm, she was able to erode many of the existing prejudices. Although some of U.L.A.E.'s less publicized prints, for example those by Grace Hartigan, are among the loveliest to have emerged from the workshop, it was Jasper Johns and Robert Rauschenberg, members of the transitional generation between Abstract Expressionism and Pop Art, who made Tanya Grosman's reputation. Eventually it may become apparent that her adoption of acceptable romantic stereotypes, together with the fact that she was uniquely able to sustain U.L.A.E.'s mythic quality, has led to a somewhat uncritical acceptance of her production. Nevertheless, she has appropriately been described as America's Vollard, and her philosophy — 'what matters is that the print be alive with the heartbeat of the artist in it'[34] — will ensure that the graphic art she produced is a lasting memorial.

TAMARIND LITHOGRAPHY WORKSHOP

While Tanya Grosman's undertaking in the early days was a decidedly hand-to-mouth affair and her technical expertise non-existent, when June Wayne created Tamarind it was as an artist who, by the late 1950s, had already extended lithographic frontiers.[1] She was also a thinker with sufficient belief in the power of the intellect first to conceptualize unerringly and then to execute efficiently a six-point plan[2] which aimed in the short term to resuscitate hand lithography in America, and in the long term to alter the ecology materially in order to ensure lithography's survival.

It is not entirely true to say, as writers are wont to do, that June Wayne and Tanya Grosman 'raised lithography from the dead'. June Wayne herself and Clinton Adams, who was first Tamarind's associate director and from 1970 Director of the Institute which succeeded it, had both practised the technique on the west coast with the printer Lynton Kistler. Similarly, Garo Antreasian was engaged on ambitious large-scale prints of up to seventeen or eighteen colours when June Wayne, who found him to be way ahead of anyone else in America, invited him to join her as Tamarind's first master printer. Nevertheless, Antreasian's lonely apprenticeship in mid-western America had depended somewhat tenuously on an enthusiastic high school teacher and a German commercial lithographer who remembered stone. Because of the effect of commercial offset on the supply of autographic materials, the possibilities for hand lithography were fast closing down rather than opening up. By 1956 — when a chemical allergy finally halted Kistler's work as a printer for artists, leaving George Miller in New York as the only printer available outside co-operative work-shops — June Wayne realized that if she wanted to continue with the kind of imagery in which she had become interested she would have to go to Europe. In 1957 she found herself in Paris, pushing the printer Marcel Durassier to help her realize the inventive washes she was making with salt on zinc for a lithographic marathon which finally ended on Christmas Day 1958 when she completed her de luxe book *John Donne: Songs and Sonets*.

June Wayne felt that American lithography was stalled by primitive materials and by a narrow range of technical accomplishment to service it. In Europe, however, although know-how about seductive washes and quality materials had survived and some major artists made original lithographs, printers were often used in a most cyni-cal way to reproduce gouaches for non-participating artists, who signed the results so they could masquerade in the expensive 'original' market.

June Wayne remembers that Durassier would refer to himself as 'nègre' (slave), or 'faux monnayeur' (counterfeiter) and would act with a great deal of arrogance; French printers 'had their own interior laughter and bitterness vis-à-vis the artist: "Oh, he acts as though he made the print. You and I know better" '.[3]

In 1958, when her mind was very much on her book, the Ford Foundation ap-proached June Wayne as one of many asked to nominate artists for grants. Although she did as requested, she added the rider that in her view there were better ways to spend money for the good of artists than by grants to individuals. Invited to elab-orate on this by the Foundation's vice-president, W. McNeil Lowry, she mentioned the plight of lithography in America and when asked to put forward a concrete proposal for measures that she felt would improve the situation, she did so as a conceptual exercise. To her surprise, the Foundation told her it would back the project only if she agreed to run it. Although it meant virtually putting her own work as an artist into cold storage, June Wayne took up the challenge out of love for the ailing process. Ten years later, when she felt her job was done and the Tamarind Institute had been set up to continue the work in a different form, she returned to her own studio.

In December 1984, when U.C.L.A. celebrated twenty-five years of Tamarind's his-tory, June Wayne reflected on how remarkable it was that anyone as powerful and special as W. McNeil Lowry 'would have heard anyone as oddball and unpowerful as I then was — a woman, an artist, a high school drop-out without recognized creden-tials, and a devotee of lithography which was about as low as you could get on the art totem pole'.[4] For his part, Lowry, showing 'rare trust in an artist's knowledge of how best to conduct an artist's affairs',[5] had been deeply impressed by June Wayne's exhaustive and graphic proposal. Although there were a lot of vested interests to contend with and the plan did not gain universal approval when circulated around America for comment, Lowry nevertheless believed in June Wayne's ability. He later said that the Foundation grant was 'a bet on one person alone'[6] — a bet that eventually netted over two million dollars for the dying craft. Clinton Adams, not one to be easily amazed, still vividly remembers his astonishment when in June 1960 he saw the professional nature of the workshop June Wayne had set up in Los Angeles.[7]

A common criticism of Tamarind encountered in the general literature is that the Workshop's educational achievements were not equalled by its aesthetic success.[8]

9 June Wayne with Josef Albers and Ken Tyler

In support of this charge, comparisons with U.L.A.E.'s production are often made. Such comparisons are rarely more than superficial, however, and have failed entirely to take account of the fact that while U.L.A.E. was a commercial publisher working in depth with a very limited group of artists (two of whom — Jasper Johns and Robert Rauschenberg — were in absolute command of the market), Tamarind's aims were very much broader. Two witty and mordant articles that June Wayne has since written about the creative process[9] and the male artist as stereotypical female[10] reveal a decidedly anti-romantic and offbeat mind, aware, in a way the conventional curator wedded to cyclical tastemaking is not, of the art market's inability to focus on more than one style at a time — despite the fact that many different aesthetics proceed concurrently. 'I have never felt it necessary to consider someone passé, in order to find somebody else new', June Wayne told an interviewer in 1976.[11] Her aim was to make it possible for a large number of artists 'to find this medium and express themselves beautifully — I felt this for the good of the art aside from a deep commitment to the idea'.[12] More importantly, she saw to it that each group of trainee printers was exposed to the complete spectrum of aesthetic ideas. She also limited artists to two months' exposure to leave them 'just a little hungry and short of satiation' in the hope that they would return to the process.

The outcome of this basic philosophy was that the artists were actually recommended by a national panel which included Harold Joachim, Gustave von Groschwitz, James Johnson Sweeney and Carl Zigrosser. In retrospect, Clinton Adams, who was also involved in the selection process, thinks that the workshop — which initially believed it had only three years to run — tried to produce too many prints in its early stages. In addition, the names put forward included too high a percentage of printmakers, since the panel was still thinking in terms of the cliché that artists paint and printmakers make prints.[13] Nevertheless, a proper assessment of Tamarind's output, free of the traditional contempt of the east coast establishment for what is done on the west coast, has yet to be undertaken. As a touchstone of the quality that emerged from the Workshop, even in its earliest days, it is interesting to compare Adja Yunkers' *Skies of Venice* with the much more often vaunted *Stones* of about the same period. The prints by Yunkers are startling for their aesthetic ambition, matched by a technical breadth that American printers were only just learning to encompass, and can hold their own with anything made in America at that time. In Hollander's opinion, June Wayne was 'as great as Tanya [Grosman] in every way . . . Tanya brought in the quality of publishing and specializing with a few artists, but June gave the nation the opportunity to really move forward into print production'.[14]

Another of the criticisms sometimes levelled against Tamarind is the fact that artists had to hand-draw their own matrices and were not allowed to use any photomechanical techniques. In 1960, this work ethic was compatible with the dominant expressionist and 'originality' conventions and was reinforced by June Wayne's desire to avoid the corrupt situation that she had found in Europe. Moreover, while there was no danger of the skills and materials attaching to photomechanical offset dying out, autographic techniques and materials were near to total extinction. Maurice Sanchez, a Tamarind trainee who now runs his own New York studio, remembers that there was resentment about this imposed limitation but admits that now, in retrospect, he knows June Wayne was right. 'It was a stifling situation', he said, 'but that is always a young person's reaction to trying to pick up a discipline. They rebel. They want to go into new techniques. They want to be hip. They think this traditional stuff is crazy. But you really need that foundation and I'm glad that they forced it down our throats'.[15]

June Wayne's ruling did affect the aesthetic intention of some artists as the 1960s progressed. The British Pop artist, Peter Phillips, whose graphic work before and since has relied almost entirely on collaged source material that has already been photomechanically processed, sat down at Tamarind for two days and hand-drew a print which has since become a curiosity within his oeuvre. Similarly, Bruce Conner, thwarted in expressing several conceptual ideas that would have required photomechanical reproduction, eventually made an image of one of his own fingerprints and another, virtually blank, entitled 'This space reserved for June Wayne'. On the other hand, to serve the hard-edge aesthetic so attuned to industrial production, Tamarind also produced the portfolios by Josef Albers with which Tyler was associated. plate 9 Although not hand-drawn by the artist, these prints nevertheless take their place among Tamarind's masterpieces.[16]

Tamarind also made a significant contribution to research which, in the long term, led to a major book on lithographic technique.[17] Projects seeking alternatives to stone and looking into autographic processes for zinc and aluminium plates — which June Wayne herself had already done so much to stimulate — were developed and methods of improving the 'chaotic impermanence' of normal lithographic inks were investigated. June Wayne repeatedly visited Europe and collaborated with manufacturers in search of stable papers.[18] She instituted research into the strain of the printing process on printers, while Clinton Adams began to formulate ethical documentation practices which, rather than trying to define the types of prints people should make, recommended complete disclosure. These pioneering landmarks provided criteria against plate 25 which others could measure their projects. As June Wayne herself put it: 'If you are walking and there isn't a tree or a fence anywhere, you never find yourself in such a flat landscape. The minute one landmark appears, then everything can relate to it'.[19]

In the end, Tamarind's achievements exceeded June Wayne's wildest dreams. By 1970, 103 artists had participated in the project and 2,900 images had been made, some of them undoubted masterpieces. Some seventy printers[20] were trained in Los Angeles, and more continued to learn when the Tamarind Institute, under the aegis of the University of New Mexico, took over the project in quite a different form, no longer financed by Ford Foundation grants. Taking the two groups of printers together, the researcher Elizabeth Jones-Popescu found in 1980 that forty-seven still printed professionally (the majority of them in their own workshops), and she claimed that only eleven percent of Tamarind's trainees had abandoned lithography.[21] The many shops set up by Tamarind printers in America have included those founded by Ken Tyler — Gemini and Tyler Graphics — plus Landfall, Chiron, Cirrus, Derrière l'Etoile, Solo, Hollanders Workshop and the Collector's Press. Tamarind printers in business further afield include Ian Lawson in England, Jürgen Fischer in Germany, and Fred Genis in Sydney, Australia. Some workshops are even employing second and third generation descendants of Tamarind. Robert Evermon, for example, one of sixty-five Tamarind-trained printers teaching in various educational institutions, taught five printers who have worked at Gemini. These printers were in turn supervised by Serge Lozingot (once Dubuffet's printer), whom June Wayne lured to America from France. Whereas there were only ten institutions teaching lithography in America in the 1950s, by 1980 there were closer to two hundred in the field.

But Tamarind did not just train printers. It made a huge contribution to the revaluation of graphic art in America and set the highest standards for professional practice in an American setting. Informed by her European experience and knowing that it improved the lustre of the result, June Wayne introduced printing on dry rather than damp paper. She encouraged an experimental environment in which American printers could develop skills to undertake the tricky counter-etching of stones, making it normal practice for an artist to be able to add, subtract and experimentally change work as proofing proceeded. She insisted also on a particular quality in the greys and her demands necessitated 'tremendous energy in the hands for printing. To keep the stone alive, meant that we were printing with a furious kind of quality control'.[22] By focusing on the role and contribution of the printer, Tamarind presented it as a real vocation, together with an important cluster of other worthwhile jobs. True collaboration, in the sense of a give and take between printer and artist, was initiated in a way that had previously existed in America only in the most marginal sense.

Aware that what happened at Tamarind would have important implications for the future of printmaking, June Wayne was concerned for the totality of her proposal. The fact that most metropolitan areas in America now have a master printer, and that as a result American artists are able to call upon the greatest range of possibilities for printmaking the world has ever known, can in very large part be traced back to her initial vision.

THE CONCEPT OF COLLABORATION

Certainly Tamarind led to a totally new profile for the sophisticated master printer who, no longer an apprenticed artisan like his counterpart in France, was now a college graduate likely to have been trained as an artist.

Such increasing specialization in the arts can be seen as a facet of the division of labour that developed with the Industrial Revolution. As art and creativity were dissociated from general manufacture, mental and manual labour came to be differentiated as a form of class distinction. Up to the sixteenth century, the words 'artist' and 'artisan' had been used indiscriminately to refer to any skilled practitioner, but as 'artist' assumed its special sense, 'artisan' gradually acquired a quite distinct meaning.[1] Interestingly enough, the definitive separation occurred in the late eighteenth century when the Royal Academy in London decided to exclude engravers from its highest ranks. An artisan then became a manual worker — skilled, yet without intellectual, imaginative or creative purpose. For although original prints have been made since printing began, the concept had not yet been defined and the engravers who were exhibited at the Academy invariably did reproductive work.

When the Tamarind Lithography Workshop reinterpreted collaboration, its maxim was that the printer should 'detect the true spirit of the work and give it life, while at the same time avoiding any act which might tend to impose his own aesthetic upon that of the artist'.[2] 'Aesthetic' may be defined as 'perceptible by the senses, as opposed to thinkable or immaterial',[3] and is usually held to be the province of the artist, although many actions taken by the printer or the publisher can become visible in the print. In fact, there is no rule which lays down that the aesthetic components of a print may not be contributed equally by both artist and printer on a fifty-fifty basis. However, since the market has been structured according to romantic ideas about originality, authenticity and authorship and since the popular view of the artist is of an individual engaged in a lonely personal struggle with materials, the idea that in special cases printers deserve equal billing — or that they may be aesthetically involved at all in the making of a print — is taboo.

Although traditional Asian and Eskimo prints record every participant, sometimes even down to the ink maker, if artistic conventions are to be upheld in the western 'democracies', the printer's contribution must be played down. For while an artist's ego must be protected, a printer is not supposed to have one. This was established a century ago, when André Mellerio criticized Vollard's printer, Auguste Clot, for substituting his own judgement when an artist's personality was not strong or assertive.[4] Many printers still interpret their function according to these rules and the world divides into those who want to believe that one cannot tell when a print comes from their workshop, and those who, like Tyler, are proud to have a particular 'look'. Similarly, the fragility of an artist's ego and dealer considerations regarding the marketability of a named product determine how much credit can be given to collaborators. For while the artist finally signs and takes responsibility for the image, however great the printer's contribution may have been, the practice of embossing a printer's chop into the paper[5] nowadays indicates, although probably only to the initiate, that others have been involved.

The problems that may ensue if an idea resides in the head of one person while its technical resolution lies in the hands of another was speculatively addressed by S. W. Hayter when he defined ideal 'originality'. Hayter analysed the components of a print as being the idea, the process of making the matrix used to realize that idea, and the printing operation itself. Certainly James McNeill Whistler's etchings provide

one obvious case of an instance where an artist felt the act of printing to be so important to the aesthetic of the work that he did not feel he could delegate it to a professional printer. All of which may suggest that technique and idea are not as unconnected as some artists, trying to differentiate their activity from that of 'printmakers', would like to believe, and that perhaps in the very greatest prints, whether or not a printer is involved, technique and idea must become indivisible.

All kinds of analogies have been used to elucidate the subtlety of the relationship that develops between artists and printers; significantly many of them are musical. For Richard Hamilton, who worked with Tyler in Bedford Village, the printer's role is passive like that of a violin with a particular tone that the artist plays. Hamilton chooses printers suitable for the image he wants to make (or, conversely, images suited to a particular printer) 'almost like casting a movie'.[6] June Wayne has also differentiated the style of one printer from another by comparing the tone of the violinist Jascha Heifetz to that of Isaac Stern — which means that she credits the printer with active interpretation. Similarly, Tanya Grosman liked to quote Barnett Newman's view of the artist as composer and the printer as performer.[7] Chris Prater, the marvellously inventive British screenprinter who worked with countless major artists in the 1960s, used the analogy of composer-conductor-orchestra for the artist, himself and his team.[8] Another image June Wayne has found appropriate is that of horse and rider, although she is well aware that there may be a question as to who is riding whom:

plate 10

> Many years ago, when I used to ride horses, I learned to trust the horse in certain terrain where its judgement was better than mine. But of course, in our societal level, the rider is responsible for the horse. In truth, I find some merit in this position, but I recognize its paradoxes as well.[9]

Garo Antreasian, Ken Tyler's teacher in Indianapolis, is one of the few to have explored the ramifications of collaboration in print from an intellectual perspective. In 1980 he wrote of the 'altruistic selflessness' sometimes demanded of and given by printers and of the fact that, as American prints had become more and more spectacular, printers were assuming an increasingly 'complex and catalytic role'.

'This role', he went on, 'is perhaps best epitomized by the master printer Ken Tyler, whose cunning and calculated utilization of present-day technological materials and processes, like the experimental outlook of Hayter in the 50s, stimulated the methodology of printmaking beyond its characteristically nineteenth-century confines'.[10]

Antreasian, who was Tamarind's first collaborative printer but has remained a prac-
tising artist, sees the question from both sides. In 1980 he had mixed feelings about
the way the collaborative process was developing, and reflected on the high public
profile of Ken Tyler compared to the no less skilful technical authority and dedication
to excellence among other printers who displayed 'greater modesty and restraint'. By
1984, however, having seen the *Swan engravings* and *Circuit* prints that Frank Stella   plates 105-108, 111
had made with Ken Tyler in the intervening years, he conceded Tyler's 'breadth of
vision' and paid him this compliment:

> The early Stellas, with the exception of the *Stars of Persia*, were not of any particular   plate 4
> significance in my view, but the last few prints that he made . . . are really major contributions
> to the whole art of printmaking and could really only have taken place through this long
> association with Ken Tyler and through a particular kind of magic that seems to develop when
> those two people get together. I think that's an example of an ideal compatibility . . . whatever
> it was that has enabled Stella to surpass his earlier efforts in printmaking by these really truly
> outstanding, dense and very inventive examples of printmaking art has a lot to do with that
> particular collaboration . . .[11]

Tyler himself discounts the role of the publisher (which he also fulfils) because
'sitting at the top, dictating down the line' only represents authority. He considers that
the most important element is contributed by the printer. Most artists, he believes:

> . . . don't know what they're doing technically. So they have to rely on the printer to advise
> them. And now the relationship starts and it's symbiotic. You can't separate it after a while
> and you don't know whether the suggestion came from the printer on the press or that it
> was the artist's idea. But you know that something's going on there and if it works, it's
> magic.[12]

Various commentators have shown an awareness that collaboration, as it has recently developed in America, represents a new degree of involvement and intensity.
In 1972 R. S. Field, curator and critic, wrote to a researcher that he realized artists
depended on these superb craftsmen 'far more than the general connoisseur, much
less the public, realizes',[13] and in a subsequent article he spoke of the indispensability
of people like Tyler who 'assume a rank almost equal to that of the artist, a creative
capacity never before experienced'.[14] Equally, John Russell, writing in *The New York
Times*, acknowledged that master printers were now able to show artists undreamed
of things, coming up with 'an end product . . . astonishing in its vigor, its assurance
and its breadth of resource'.[15]

TYLER ON THE WEST COAST 1963-1973

TYLER'S TRAINING

Kenneth E. Tyler was born in 1931 in East Chicago, Indiana, on the south shore of Lake Michigan, a town where Shell, Sinclair and Standard turn crude oil into gasoline. His parents, Paul and Elizabeth Tyler, were Hungarian immigrants who had changed their name from Tyira when they arrived in America in 1915; Paul Tyler was a steel worker. During the difficult years of the Depression, Tyler was obliged to pick up coal in the railway yards to heat the family house.[1] Although his parents gave him general encouragement to 'rise above the level they just came from', there was no encouragement as far as art was concerned. It was in fact a music teacher who inspired Tyler to take up a scholarship to the Art Institute of Chicago, where he studied for a Bachelor's degree in Art Education. One component of his course of study was the rather limited form of lithography typical of the time, taught by Max Kahn.

To help pay for his education, Tyler did summer work shovelling iron ore and galvanizing nuts and bolts. However, he also helped to mount prints at the Art Institute where, among other things, he fell in love with the lithographs of Odilon Redon. In 1952 he won a scholarship to the Sorbonne in Paris, but, due to the outbreak of the Korean war, found himself instead at an officers' training school for the Engineers' Corps. From 1954 he worked part-time for a scenic studio constructing sets for ballet and opera, before taking up a position teaching art at Evanston Township High School — where he also helped build a million dollar auditorium. Next, he moved up the company ladder as an employee of a specialty strip steel manufacturer. There he was introduced to metallurgy, to Dale Carnegie salesmanship and to the responsibility for developing industrial techniques for corporate inventions.

By 1962, married and 'drinking too many martinis',[2] Tyler decided something was missing. Feeling a need to get back into contact with art, he enrolled for a Master's degree at the John Herron School in Indianapolis where Garo Antreasian taught lithography. He told an audience at a paper conference in March 1978 that he could still recall his excitement at seeing the very large stones on which Antreasian was working and the prints he had made from them.[3] This first encounter with a scale unusual for the time is of critical importance, because large prints were to become part of Tyler's credo. He felt that to attract the energies of major artists, works of graphic art had to be able to take their place alongside paintings on the wall, and he still believes that increasing the size of prints has been one of his most important contributions to printmaking. His experience in Indianapolis also made him realize that he was never happier than when he was using his hands and led to his determination to put his 'whole heart and soul into being a printer'.[4]

It was through Antreasian that Tyler was offered a Ford Foundation Fellowship to the Tamarind Lithography Workshop in 1963. During his first year at Tamarind Irwin plate 9 Hollander was the master printer there. From 1964 to 1965 Tyler took over that role and served as the Workshop's technical director. While he admitted recently that Tamarind was 'the stepping-stone for me to go into my commercial life as a printer and publisher',[5] there were aspects of the philosophy there that Tyler reacted against.

Although the job on which she focused was hand lithography, it would be difficult to find someone less romantic or more professional about her work than June Wayne. Yet Tyler often implied that at Tamarind they were 'hopeless craft romantics'.[6] He said they were 'too precious' and 'never did have the sensibility for technological advance'[7] (which, he insisted, *was* a sensibility). In an article of 1977, in which Judith Goldman reported that he had decided in 1963 to concentrate on research and techniques, Tyler was quoted as saying that: 'At Tamarind they didn't know anything about it'.[8] They clearly knew enough to engage technical directors.

While Tyler may have gone further and faster than many of his contemporaries, it was at the Herron School and at Tamarind that he first encountered the many aspects of print research that he was later to develop.

Garo Antreasian, for example, who was interested in bringing lithography into the twentieth century, had designed a press using hydraulics that was working reliably in Indianapolis by 1963, the year Tyler studied at Herron. In 1965 Tyler had his own hydraulic designs custom built, arriving at a model with both hydraulic bed and hy- plate 11 draulic scraper bar system. This innovation allowed for a flow smoother than the staccato movement of a hand press and permitted Tyler to print flats without marks in them, which was a considerable technical advance.

11 Tyler operating his new hydraulic press at Gemini Ltd in 1965 during the editioning of Nicholas Krushenick's *Fairfax and mustard*

Since its inception, Tamarind had also been aware of the need for substitute printing surfaces, and while training there Tyler worked with Harris Intertype on ball-grained aluminium plates that could be printed alongside images from stone without jarring

contrast. He would also eventually develop a deep interest in paper, a subject that June Wayne herself had extensively explored. As Antreasian pointed out at a paper conference in 1978, the Tamarind Archive in New Mexico contains no fewer than fifty separate binders that deal exhaustively with the subject of papers suitable for lithography and reveal 'the singular vision, passion and persistence' of the Workshop's founder.[9]

Indeed, Garo Antreasian and another of Tamarind's principals, Clinton Adams, based what is now known as the 'bible' of the direct lithographic process — *The Tamarind Book of Lithography* — on the multifaceted technical research conducted at the Lithography Workshop by a whole succession of printer and curator trainees. The book credits Tyler with information about printing from metal plates using photomechanical procedures that he later developed in his own workshop.

Tamarind also provided a meeting place that proved of primary importance for Tyler's career. Marcel Durassier, the French printer with whom June Wayne had worked in 1958, visited Tamarind in August 1963 and he and Tyler established an instant rapport. The Frenchman told Tyler that 'destiny had thrown them together' (although, in fact, 'destiny' should once again read 'Tamarind'). Tyler's notes about Durassier exude an emotion that makes obvious how much inspiration he derived from the encounter.[10]

Durassier spoke of lithography as 'an old goat' but communicated an unwavering devotion to it. Working on zinc and on stone, he criticized some American chemicals and processes, adversely compared the thick chamfer of the maple scraper bars on the local presses with fine ones made of wild dogwood from his native France, and swapped arcane formulae, such as that for a fountain etch he called 'Devil's water', containing, among other things, a pint of white wine and some lemon juice. He also divulged a range of technical tricks, such as a method of regrinding small areas of a stone with a cuttle bone after corrections and he convinced Tyler of the necessity of preserving greys accurately and of keeping the stone 'alive', whatever one felt of the work of the artist for whom one was printing. Durassier demonstrated how to ink a stone 'with great love', favouring the greys and rolling slowly, using his wrists. Most of all, he imparted a sense of the struggle necessary in the creative life, and the idea that, however much one knew, there was always something to learn, some standard of excellence at which to aim. Tyler responded very powerfully to this idea. When he declined the Frenchman's invitation to work in France because of his family commitments, Durassier ceremonially presented him with his roller in a way Tyler describes as 'almost like a religious laying-on of hands'.[11]

If Tyler later hammered home his philosophical differences with Tamarind with somewhat aggressive fervour, his reasons doubtless stemmed from his belief that you only learn 'where there is no ceiling', and from the need he felt to proselytize for what the print world would later call 'a future-oriented industrial aesthetic' that 'Americanized the concept of the artisan printer'.[12]

As he explained a decade later:

> By 1964 it became clear to me that most traditional methods, as well as some recent practices of the hand-printing crafts, were not compatible with the images of major contemporary artists. As a collaborator I left the ranks of this revival to aid the major artist in his search for new graphic expression and new work environments.[13]

While an 'industrial aesthetic' had been in evidence before, Tyler had accurately sensed that the artists of the early 1960s were making a major assault on the intervening expressionist/originality conventions, not only in America, but elsewhere. For example, the British screenprinter Chris Prater, of Kelpra Studio, who made his first print for an artist in 1961,[14] had by the mid-sixties produced a remarkable body of work for a number of painters representing the new hard-edge and Pop Art developments. Tyler greatly admired this British work and, although it was created using a different technique, he saw it as an important parallel to his own:

I was very fond of Chris Prater of Kelpra Studio and felt his achievements in screenprinting in the early sixties were major graphic statements. The prints he made with Ron Kitaj, Richard Hamilton, Eduardo Paolozzi and Joe Tilson were brilliant. He, in my opinion, singlehandedly moved screenprinting from a commercial medium to a fine art form. I have great respect for the printer collaboration that took place there. I asked him in the late sixties to join my workshop in Los Angeles if he wanted to. I felt we shared a common love of perfection and technological achievements. I felt we would be a helluva team. But that didn't work out . . .[15]

Although the screenprints Prater had made were celebrated in exhibitions of 1970[16] and 1980[17] and eventually formed the kernel of the Tate Gallery's contemporary print collection, his work was vilified when it first appeared. Exhibited at the Biennale des Jeunes in Paris in 1965, at a time when the 1937 original print definition outlawing photoprocess had just been reiterated in *Nouvelles de l'Estampe*,[18] six works made at Kelpra, one of which displayed the dreaded photographic half-tone dot, were segregated by French officials from the 'handmade' prints. Although the Print Council of America definition did not mention photography and was never quite so proscriptive as those formulated in Europe, it nevertheless insisted that 'the artist alone should create the master image'. Even an historian as broadly based as Carl Zigrosser, who supported the Council's position in a publication of 1965/6, interpreted the new hard-edge and 'Pop' imagery, too familiar and banal to be taken seriously, as the death knell of 'the original print'. Too close to events to recognize that impersonal techniques and photomechanical quotations were fundamental to the aesthetic of some contemporary artists, Zigrosser believed that they were falling back on such processes because they were impatient with the 'drudgery' involved in traditional prints; 'mass man', he suggested, would not balk at mass-produced images.[19]

JOSEF ALBERS

plate 12

Josef Albers is the quintessential example of an artist whose mature graphic work made little use of his personal touch. Tyler's meeting with him was yet another important introduction made possible by Tamarind, for, as he later observed, the artist became 'the catalyst of my career'.[1] Already in his seventies and grateful for the work Tamarind had done on three *Interlinear* prints in 1962, Albers returned in late 1963 to make the *Day and night* portfolio based on the same theme as his *Homage to the square* paintings. While the format of a square within a square looks simplicity itself, there is nothing in the world more difficult to print than a precise area of uninflected colour; it requires infinite patience and the dedication of a printer who perpetually practises his craft. Nor is this so-called industrial aesthetic, the first wave of which emerged between the wars, as machine-made and unemotional as it superficially looks. A critic writing of similar prints exhibited in 1922 by Albers' Bauhaus colleague Moholy Nagy, aptly described them as 'sensuality refined to its most sublimated expression'.[2] Coolness is therefore relative; it is not so much that flat colour is impersonal, as that the personality must be sought somewhere other than in obvious handling.

Albers was such a perfectionist that to obtain the particular colour he desired often meant mixing thirty-five different blues only to discard them all. 'I accepted it as a challenge . . . I adored the activity',[3] Tyler said. The challenge for Tyler in *Day and night* was to overprint two inks to make a third colour and achieve transparency without surface reflection. He managed to do this by blotting the second colour immediately after printing, a trick he had learned from his own earlier work in Indianapolis.

12 Ken Tyler with Josef Albers at the Tamarind Lithography Workshop, Los Angeles, in 1963

13 Albers and Tyler discussing the *White embossing on gray series* of 1971 at the artist's studio in Connecticut

In 1964 Albers returned to Tamarind to make the eight monochromatic lithographs entitled *Midnight and noon*, where the same ink in two different densities produced three colour variants. Albers wanted to capitalize on inks, thinned but not mixed, so that a full black could, as he put it in a letter of June 1964, 'permit numerous steps of density between the thinnest light grey to a deep velvet'. He went on:

> I hope you can try already some inks and see whether only thinning and diluting will do it. Or we *must* use white (which I would like to avoid) or mix ourselves our hoped-for double-faced inks. Or, or, or, we make all the prints so extremely thin, as nobody dared before. Anyway, it appears adventurous, thank heaven.
>
> Yours Josef.[4]

Once again, Tyler pulled off the difficult task, proofing the eight prints for the portfolio. As Clinton Adams put it: 'Tyler and Albers were the ideal collaborative relationship. Ken's basic temperament as a printer is for cleanness, clarity, crispness. All of these adjectives describe stylistic characteristics of Albers' work . . . They meshed just perfectly'.[5]

In July 1965, after the prints were completed, Albers was depressed by an article on originality that Katherine Kuh had written in *The Saturday Review*.[6] He discussed his concerns in a letter to June Wayne, who in reply comforted him:

> Your lithos are original in every sense. There is no way for the Print Council or anyone else to imply anything else. I wouldn't fret if I were you.
>
> When Balanchine creates a ballet, must he perform every leap himself? No, the dancers are his tools . . .[7]

plates 17-20

The issue of originality was hotly debated throughout the mid-sixties. While he was working on *White line squares*, Albers, in a taped discussion between himself, Tyler and Henry T. Hopkins (then of the Los Angeles County Museum), remembered how June Wayne had supported him. And he went on to say that Theodore Gusten of the Print Council of America, 'a fanatic of the right rules' who believed all artists should make their own plates, had not liked it much when he had confessed that: 'I never touch the stone, never the rule, never the ink, it's all done by my friend Ken, but I watch him like Hell...'[8] In fact, as Albers told Hopkins, Tyler's 'controlled hands made possible what his seventy-eight year old bones could not do. 'I'm shivering [trembling] you know', he said.

His experiences with Albers and Durassier convinced Tyler that he had a talent for printing and that he should go into business for himself. He abandoned his personal Tamarind chop, in which his initials created a form like a scarab beetle, and adopted as the chop for his own publishing house the sign of the zodiac for Gemini, the heavenly twins. When Albers asked him, years later, how he came to use this sign, Tyler told him that it symbolized things in pairs — for example, the water and grease in lithography, or the artist and the printer in collaboration. Gemini was also associated with the American aerospace programme, in connection with which the most futuristic technology in the world was unfolding.

plate 11

Tyler set up shop at 8221 Melrose Avenue, Los Angeles, employing another ex-Tamarind printer, Bernard Bleha. The first artist with whom they worked was Nicholas Krushenick, who made a fund-raising print for the Los Angeles County Museum. Tyler also worked with John Altoon, who lived next door to the workshop. Together they published the book *About women* with the poet Robert Creeley. Tyler told a panel discussion in 1975[9] that making the book had been 'absolute heaven', since each collaborator wanted only the other's happiness and neither had ever asked how much money was going to be generated by the project. 'I never had a repeat of that in my life', Tyler said. When he hurt his back, Altoon was 'fantastic', taking him to the Beverly Hills Health Club and generally helping with his recuperation. The episode lends a special poignancy to Tyler's prescription for a printer — 'a strong back, a young inquisitive mind and a feel for beauty'.[10]

David Hockney, another artist Tyler had met at Tamarind, worked with him for the London publisher Editions Alecto on a witty series about an imaginary collector's group of six pictures — among them *Picture of a landscape in an elaborate gold frame* and *Picture of a pointless abstraction framed under glass*. Gemini Ltd. was housed behind a framing business and Hockney later told *London Life* that seeing all the marvellous frames in the window gave him the idea for a set of *trompe l'oeil* pictures within pictures.

plate 16

plates 14-15

On 1 February 1966, Tyler, interested in extending his publishing activity rather than the contract printing side of the business, formed a corporation with two business men and art enthusiasts — Sidney B. Felsen, an accountant (who from 1968 worked at Gemini full time) and Stanley Grinstein, owner of a fork-lift business. Tyler told a researcher in 1973 that the business acumen of his two partners was of 'inestimable value' in helping him to realize his creative dreams. The new company retained the name of Gemini, but added G.E.L. (Graphic Editions Ltd.) to differentiate it from its predecessor. Although Tyler directed the shop, his two partners met with him regularly to discuss projects and were often roped in to help.[11]

plates 3-4

Gemini G.E.L.'s first publication, four-fifths of the proceeds from which Albers gave to help fund the new company, was the artist's seventeen-print sequence of *White line squares*. At Tamarind, Albers had given Tyler a design on graph paper dated 28 October 1963. It was for a 20¾" square, marked off in the proportions of various possible configurations of the *Homage to the square* series, based on concentric squares displaced on one axis. 'It's only the dish I serve my craziness about colour in', Albers said.[12] He inscribed the diagram 'For Ken, my excellent helper', and the drawing authorized Tyler to make plates based on it for the artist whenever requested. What made the *White line squares* much harder to perfect than the Tamarind prints (which were difficult enough) was the fact that colours had to be abutted without overlap. The theory behind the suite, inspired by the extensive work the artist had done on the relativity of colour, was that if one of three interlocking colour areas is divided by a fine white line it produces an illusion of two colours making a total percept of four. 'It's so exciting', enthused Albers when he saw some of the early proofs. 'Color fools you all the time.'[13]

plates 19-20

Tyler had to achieve the immaculate precision necessary with papers that stretched in the press and with coloured inks that each had a differing capacity for expansion. His brilliant solution was to minutely shrink or enlarge his rubylith stencils of the basic shapes by the way he differentially burned them into the photolitho plates. It took him nine months to perfect the technique and to arrive at exact colour proofs based on colour samples that Albers painted and cut in half, keeping one half in his studio and sending the other to Gemini. It took another eight months to edition the work. The most remarkable thing about this act of collaboration was that it was supervised long distance by way of letters, phone calls, and charts sent from Tyler on the west coast to Albers on the east. Frequent telephone conversations were tape-recorded and survive in transcript. These tapes were made partly because Tyler noticed a high 'psychological fallout' on the part of the printers, Jim Webb and Bernard Bleha, who were alienated by the look of the honed-in hard edges and flat thin colours which had to be printed without roller marks or blemishes of any sort. To counteract the printers' sense of alienation and to bring them closer to Albers, Tyler played them the recordings of his conversations with the artist:

plate 17

A lot of my nit-picking and struggle to have a very· high standard in the printing was taken now with a better attitude because they heard the great joy from Albers when he saw a beautiful proof or a beautiful color. I think that made a profound difference in the attitude of our little workshop. It certainly started us off with the right idea, that nothing was impossible and that the artist should really be in total control and that the demanding of better and better quality in the printing was absolutely essential and something that should be expected.[14]

When Albers asked how 'the boys' liked his stuff, Tyler was able to reply: 'They

14 David Hockney: *Picture of a pointless abstraction framed under glass* from *A Hollywood collection*, 1965, 30 x 22 in (76.2 x 55.8 cm), lithograph, edition 85

15 David Hockney: *Picture of a landscape in an elaborate gold frame* from *A Hollywood collection*, details as No. 14

16 David Hockney drawing an aluminium plate for a lithograph from the suite *A Hollywood collection*, 1965

14

15

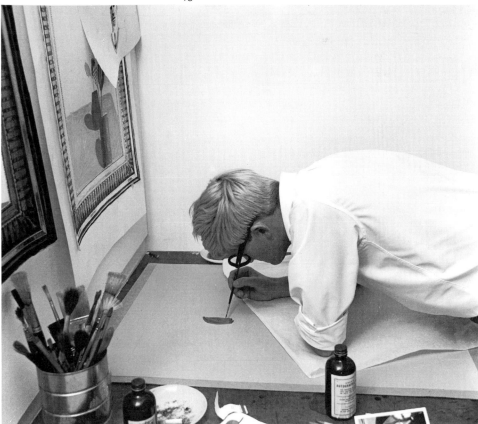

16

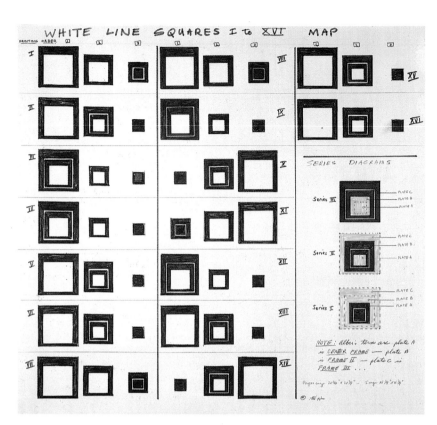

17   Josef Albers and Kenneth Tyler:
Diagram showing printing order for
White line squares I-XVI, February 1966,
19 x 20 in (48.2 x 50.8 cm), fibre-tipped
pen, coloured pencil, ballpoint pen

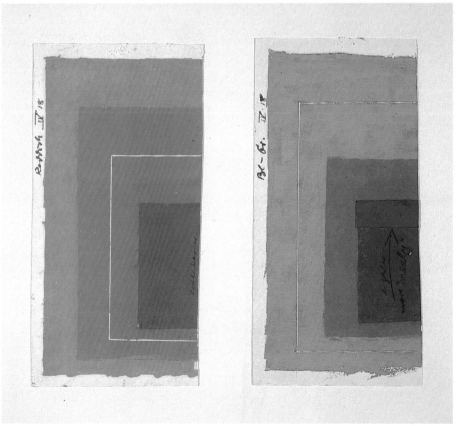

18   Josef Albers: oil studies for *White
line squares*, 1966

19 Josef Albers: *White line square XI*,
1966, 21 x 21 in (53.3 x 53.3 cm), lithograph,
edition 125

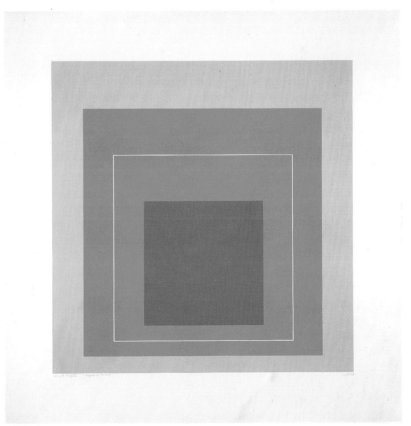

20 Josef Albers: *White line square XVI*,
1966, 21 x 21 in (53.3 x 53.3 cm), lithograph,
edition 125

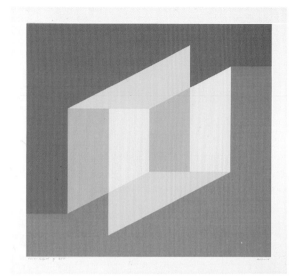

love it. It's a real challenge, Josef. I think we have done a great deal for lithography'. 'It's remarkable', said Albers. 'It's now so convincing. It's because of you.'[15]

In 1969 Albers worked again with Gemini to produce his *Embossed linear constructions*. Having proved the instability of colour, the artist proceeded to demonstrate yet again the relativity of visual phenomena by a kind of geometric surrealism in which straight lines exhibited the most illogical possibilities. This time, the drawings went through endless refinements before an engineering programmer translated them into a digital mylar tape capable of directing an automatic engraving mill. This mill cut the printing plates for an edition of pristine inkless embossings; similar embossings combined with a grey colour flat were used in the *White embossings on gray* of 1971.

Until his death in 1976 at the age of eighty-eight, Albers remained faithful to Tyler. When Tyler went east, the artist once again came to his aid, working with him exclusively in the new Bedford Village facility to screenprint the two exquisite portfolios, *Gray instrumentation I* and *II*. These were the first screenprinted portfolios Albers had made in which the squares did not overlap but were abutted; Tyler devised another ingenious registration system using pins mounted in thê bed of the press. Once again, invoking science in the service of poetry, Albers made the allegedly hard edges of the squares magically disappear and dissolve.

The year Albers died, Tyler managed to complete for him two more portfolios — *Mitered squares* and *Never before*. The latter employed an image Albers had hardly used in painting which suggested a proscenium seen through the wings of a stage, on which the colours danced. Now a regular visitor to Bedford Village, which was close to his home in Connecticut, Albers would bring in leaves as colour references

21 Josef Albers: screenprint from the portfolio *Never before*, 1976, 19 x 20 in (48.2 x 50.8 cm), edition 46

22 Josef Albers: *White embossing on gray I*, 1971, 26 x 20 in (66.0 x 50.8 cm), embossed line-cut, edition 125

plates 13, 22, 24

plate 25

plates 21, 23

23 Josef Albers, screenprint from the *Mitered squares* portfolio, 1975, 19 x 19 in (48.2 x 48.2 cm), edition 36

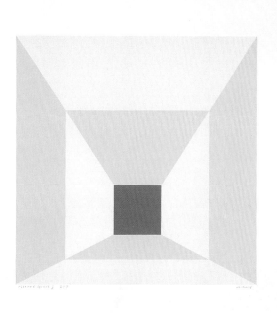

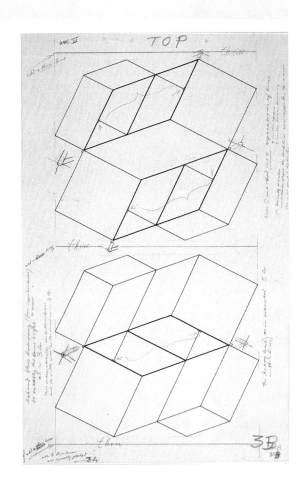

24 Preliminary drawing for *White embossing on gray VI*, *c*.1970, with working notes by Albers in fibre-tipped pen and pencil

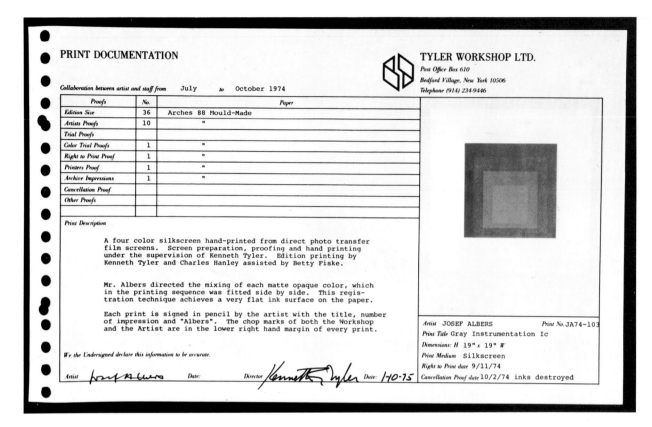

PRINT DOCUMENTATION

TYLER WORKSHOP LTD.
Post Office Box 610
Bedford Village, New York 10506
Telephone (914) 234-9446

Collaboration between artist and staff from   July   to   October 1974

Proofs	No.	Paper
Edition Size	36	Arches 88 Mould-Made
Artists Proofs	10	"
Trial Proofs		
Color Trial Proofs	1	"
Right to Print Proof	1	"
Printers Proof	1	"
Archive Impressions	1	"
Cancellation Proof		
Other Proofs		

Print Description

A four color silkscreen hand-printed from direct photo transfer
film screens. Screen preparation, proofing and hand printing
under the supervision of Kenneth Tyler. Edition printing by
Kenneth Tyler and Charles Hanley assisted by Betty Fiske.

Mr. Albers directed the mixing of each matte opaque color, which
in the printing sequence was fitted side by side. This registration technique achieves a very flat ink surface on the paper.

Each print is signed in pencil by the artist with the title, number
of impression and "Albers". The chop marks of both the Workshop
and the Artist are in the lower right hand margin of every print.

We the Undersigned declare this information to be accurate.

Artist _(signature)_   Date: Director _(signature)_ Date: 1-10-75

Artist JOSEF ALBERS   Print No. JA74-103
Print Title Gray Instrumentation Ic
Dimensions: H 19" x 19" W
Print Medium Silkscreen
Right to Print date 9/11/74
Cancellation Proof date 10/2/74 inks destroyed

and would take the printers outside to show them trees against the sky. Tyler was
glad that he had been able to realize these portfolios for the artist before he died. He
said of Albers:

> He stirred my imagination, influenced me, and above all loved giving me a challenge and
> being there to cheer and praise me on. He was a very good friend, a teacher and an
> exceptional mentor. In the thirteen years I worked with him, I never knew him not expressing
> his profound love for art, for craft, and for the work struggle that creative people are involved
> with. Money, success and power were not of concern to Josef.[16]

25 Documentation sheet
for Josef Albers, *Gray
instrumentation*, 1974,
from Tyler's Bedford
Village workshop

ROBERT RAUSCHENBERG

Despite his reverence for Albers and the increasing fame that the artist enjoyed as he approached the end of his life, Tyler knows that it was his success in attracting the two superstars of the 1960s art world — Jasper Johns and Robert Rauschenberg — that really cemented Gemini's reputation, just as they were also responsible for Tanya Grosman's success at U.L.A.E.

When the Gemini exhibition *Technics and Creativity* opened at the Museum of Modern Art in 1971 and drew such swingeing criticism, these 'stars', among others, were the focus of the attack. The artists were accused of using the press to make reproductions, the press was accused of dominating art by technique, and both were charged with doing it only for the money. In the *New York Times*, David Shirey, whose critique followed an even more virulent attack by Hilton Kramer four days earlier, wrote of 'the thick ether of staleness' and 'the miasma of commercialism' and said that the technique 'either caused havoc on the work or considerably diminished its expression'. Although six years later he had forgotten how to spell Mrs Grosman's name and had decided that June Wayne and Ken Tyler had also helped graphic art achieve its new level of expression, at the time of *Technics and Creativity* Shirey declared that neither Gemini nor Tamarind 'approaches the Tatyana Grosman workshop which is devoted to quality'.[1] Judith Goldman, Tyler's faithful chronicler, managed a more balanced account, but she too considered that Johns' Gemini prints 'lack the precise subtlety that made his U.L.A.E. prints so distinctive'.[2]

The cliché that eventually found its way into the folklore is typified by Theodore Donson's observation that:

> Gemini printers eschewed traditional hand lithography while that process was being evangelized by June Wayne and old-world craftsmanship was being romanticized by Tatyana Grosman, preferring to take advantage of whatever transfer or photomechanical technique, device, or short-cut secured the pictorial effect sought by the artist . . .[3]

While it was true that Tyler embraced new methods avidly, it was in fact the beautiful traditional washes achieved by lithographers of the late nineteenth century (which he realized had often been printed in long and far from precious editions) that drew him to lithography in the first place. Moreover, while at Tamarind, he had expanded some of the traditional techniques for drawing on stone, chiefly by means of a procedure known as 'acid-tint' which he developed for Robert Hansen's book, *Satan's saint*. Serge Lozingot, who followed Tyler as master printer at Gemini, criticized his predecessor's washes as 'foggy',[4] but the artist and Tamarind master printer John Sommers took a very different view. Describing 'acid-tint' as a method resembling aquatint that entailed working back with acid through ink rubbed into the artist's image on the stone, Sommers commented that Hansen must have been gratified to see the enormously enriched grey scale and 'the soft velvety and fine grained textures'[5] that Tyler had obtained from the artist's lithographic drawings.

The continual talk of an industrial aesthetic and cool, depersonalized, flat and immaculate surfaces (which characteristics some Gemini prints undoubtedly did display) concealed the fact that many of the traditional values were also present. In many ways, Tyler's precision and fine tuning (leading to hundreds of discarded proofs in the case of Albers, for example) actually took a higher degree of printer dedication than sensuous washes, although if Johns and Rauschenberg had not found what they wanted at Gemini, they would hardly have returned there year after year. As a matter of fact, Tyler later said that he had not expected them to return to his shop after the reception given to *Technics and Creativity*.

There was irony too in the fact that the *New York Times* castigated Gemini for working with 'very well-known or very well-connected artists'.[6] Only artists with a certain standing in the market can justify, by the price their work commands, the man-hours that a company such as Gemini invests in each project. Then, like U.L.A.E., Tyler was also responding to W. S. Lieberman's view that only great artists made great prints. Tyler had heard Lieberman give a lecture to that effect at the University of Southern California in 1964 and in subsequent discussion was told: 'It doesn't matter how much you improve technique — great prints are only made by great artists'. Nevertheless, Tyler always hoped that his concentration on research and development would enable artists to make more than 'a signature print'[7] and that opportunities to expand the various media would lead to something far more ambitious than anything which could be achieved in their own studios or even in other graphic workshops.

'What we do', he told a researcher in 1973, 'is commission major artists, tell them the sky's the limit, do anything they want to do . . . we encourage the artists to make demands on the medium. The artist's opinion is of the utmost importance to us. When the artist says "jump", we jump and when he says "junk" we junk'.[8]

It was after consulting W. S. Lieberman that Tanya Grosman invited Jasper Johns to make prints on Long Island in 1960, and Robert Rauschenberg two years later. The two artists formed a bridge between Abstract Expressionism and the Pop generation of the 1960s. When Johns first showed his work in New York in 1958, the exhibition was an immediate sensation and all the paintings — banal images, such as targets, numbers and flags, sensitively handled in the unusual wax medium of encaustic — sold out. Rauschenberg was already the 'enfant terrible' of the art world when his most notorious 'combine painting', *Monogram* — the tyre-girdled Angora goat standing on a freely brushed horizontal canvas — caused another furore the following year. Suddenly heroism and high art were out of fashion and the Abstract Expressionists found themselves superseded. The rising generation of Pop artists rejected the abstract expressionist manipulation of paint in favour of cool smooth surfaces, but Johns and Rauschenberg, while introducing the kind of imagery that was to become a hallmark of Pop, both retained a painterly style.

Rauschenberg began to make lithographs at U.L.A.E. somewhat reluctantly, thinking that the twentieth century was 'no time to start writing on rocks'.[9] Eventually, however, he fell in love with working on limestone which he said 'had all the frailty and sensitivity of an albino skin'.[10] Following a new practice in painting, Rauschenberg's lithographs united painterly lithographic washes with photographic images derived from disused printers' engraving plates from the *New York Times*. These were inked in tusche and then printed down onto the stone, so that they were partly hand-made and partly 'mechanical'. As Riva Castleman put it, Rauschenberg's compositions were 'stroboscopically choreographed' so that the material would be sensed 'in the same manner as the eye senses the total environment'.[11]

Rauschenberg's first project for Gemini in 1967 was a set of eight prints entitled *Booster and 7 studies* which 'virtually redefined the possibilities of size and scale in contemporary prints'.[12] *Booster*, which was six feet (182.9 cm) high, incorporated full length X-ray shots of the artist, nude but for his hobnailed boots. The photographic elements were developed on sensitized plates, printed onto transfer paper and then set down onto two separate stones, because no stone was large enough by itself. Eventually the image was printed one half at a time onto a single sheet of paper that had been specially developed for Tyler's project. Tyler, who said that to work with Rauschenberg was to 'get his life, spirit, energy', was grateful that the artist was 'prepared to commit large-scale ideas unselfishly to the print medium'.[13] *Booster* was much publicized at the time as the largest hand-pulled lithograph ever made in America, although the artist added another foot to his own record during his *Stoned moon* project. After the four lithographic colours on *Booster* were completed, an astronomical chart for 1967 was screenprinted in red over the entire image by a

plate 26

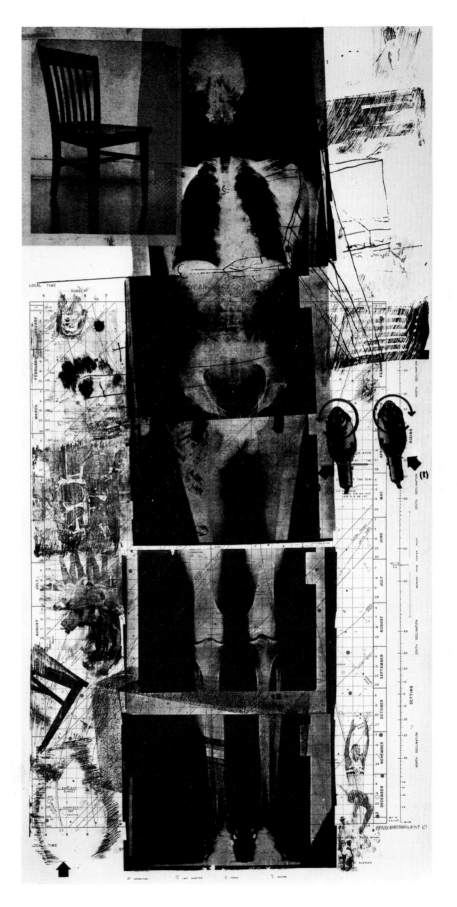

26 Robert Rauschenberg: *Booster* from
Booster and 7 studies, 1967, 72 x 35½ in
(182.8 x 90.1 cm), lithograph,
screenprint, edition 38

27 Robert
Rauschenberg: *Local
means* from the *Stoned
moon series*, 1970, 32½ x
43½ in (82.5 x 110.4 cm),
lithograph, edition 11

nearby commercial printer, Jeff Wasserman. Wasserman, who had been subcon-
tracted for the job, barely knew who Rauschenberg was at the time, and superimposing the red chart over the entire edition took him only eighteen minutes. 'Afterwards',
Tyler quipped in a panel discussion sixteen years later, 'they picked me off the floor
and gave me cardiac arrest therapy!'.[14]

In 1969 Douglas Davis expressed the opinion that through lithography the artist had
reached the peak of his work in two dimensions. Davis dated the breakthrough to the
Gemini prints of February 1967.[15] Rauschenberg's work on the *Booster and 7
studies*, he said, had been 'very nearly mythologized'. As at West Islip, Rauschenberg
welcomed friends and strangers to Gemini, conversing as he dealt with up to four or
five stones at a time. He finished his series in two and a half weeks of almost continuous effort.

While U.L.A.E. always tended to be a leisurely one-print-at-a-time affair, the atmosphere, location and scale of the operation at Gemini encouraged working in series.
Rauschenberg treated the whole experience rather like one of his performances and
the printers were totally integrated into his spontaneous activity. In fact the artist said
later that the thing he liked best about printmaking:

> . . . which refers back to the non-ego approach to life, is that printmaking is a collaboration:
> not only with people, but with materials too. I'm a strong believer that two people having good
> ideas can produce more together than two people with good ideas working separately.
> Collaboration not only takes the self-consciousness out of the artist, but the total result is
> generally so much greater, almost immeasurably.[16]

The prints Rauschenberg produced were affected by alternating periods at Gemini

28 Robert Rauschenberg: *Banner* from the *Stoned moon series*, 1969, 54½ x 36 in (138.4 x 91.4 cm), lithograph, edition 40

on the west coast and U.L.A.E. in the east, for Gemini's efforts encouraged U.L.A.E. to try fresh technological strategies. Back in West Islip after the completion of *Booster*, the artist was shown a more direct method for making transfers from magazine images onto the stone borrowing some ideas from his own *Dante* drawings of 1959. The new method was actually discovered by Bill Goldston, later to become U.L.A.E.'s master printer. Goldston was a student of Zigmunds Priede in Minneapolis and at this time Priede also printed occasionally for Tanya Grosman. As he was drafted into the army in the summer of 1967, Goldston was not able to work with Rauschenberg himself, but his discovery was passed on to the artist who used it for three eerily transparent lithographs in faded, subfusc colours — the absolute antithesis of the Gemini prints. In 1968, following a commission for a *Time* magazine cover based on the movie *Bonnie and Clyde*, Rauschenberg was back at Gemini. There he made *Reels (B + C)* in gory and fluorescent colours, capturing the gaudiness and sentimentality of the film in a burst of sixty-four hours of continuous activity from 14 to 16 January. The difference between the two shops is underlined by the fact that while Gemini published this set of six Los Angeles prints within three months, one of the U.L.A.E. prints that had been created much earlier had not yet appeared. While in the east reflection and introspection were encouraged, the emphasis in the west was on keeping the artist's momentum and excitement flowing.

In 1969 Rauschenberg inaugurated new premises for Gemini (three blocks down the road) with a very extensive series of thirty-three lithographs celebrating America's moon landing. The artist was invited by the National Aeronautics and Space Administration (NASA) to watch the Apollo II spacecraft take off from Cape Canaveral in July. Rauschenberg used official photographs of the event for a group of prints ranging from the immense and colourful *Sky garden*, capturing the moment of blast-off and 89 inches (226 cm) high, to the small monochrome *Sky rite,* which, rather than celebrating the astronauts, applauds the ground staff who made such a mission possible. Rauschenberg pressed every kind of image into service — diagrams, maps and photographs — linking them together with the familiar crayon scribble and tusche washes. The photographs were translated into print in a variety of ways, including the use of photosensitized stones which U.L.A.E. had pioneered the same summer, although not without some problems, caused by the emulsion lifting. The *Stoned moon* prints juxtapose everyday images of normality — birds, oranges, the official seal of the state plates 27-29 of Florida — with the science-fiction quality of the event. Photographs linked by manual gesture suggest the interaction between man and machine and communicate the momentous nature of the moonshot, which also moved Rauschenberg to write a poetic text:

> The bird's nest bloomed with fire and clouds. Softly largely slowly silently Apollo 11 started to move up. Then it rose being lifted on light. Standing mid-air, it began to sing happily loud. In its own joy wanting the earth to know it was going. Saturated, super-saturated and solidified air with a sound that became your body. For that while everything was the same material. Power over power joy pain ecstasy. There was no inside, no out. Then bodily transcending a state of energy, Apollo 11 was airborne, lifting pulling everyone's spirits with it.[17]

Lawrence Alloway found the series 'a technological equivalent of Rubens' *Medici cycle* . . . in its pomp, wit and fidelity'.[18] In terms of collaboration, it proved a marathon for the printers. For two months, the shop worked from fourteen to sixteen hours a day and such was the intensity of effort that, true to Rauschenberg's form, a number of stones were broken. Tyler told a reporter that the printers had actually slept at Gemini or wherever they could stretch out, and 'neither the artist nor a press was ever left unattended, because the place became essential to Rauschenberg's creative juices'.[19] The printers exulted in the part they were able to play and at the end of the project Rauschenberg generously made *Local means*, borrowing elements from the plate 27

29 The artist looks on as Ken Tyler and Charles Ritt (foreground) process lithographic stones for his *Stoned moon* series, 1969

top of *Sky garden*, as a special thank-you to the eleven who had collaborated with him.

Until Rauschenberg arrived at Gemini, the workshop's choice of artists tended to be conservative, with Edward Hopper, Hans Hofmann and Ben Shahn among those unsuccessfully approached. In fact, like Tanya Grosman, Tyler initially wanted to attract the older generation of Abstract Expressionists — Willem de Kooning, Franz Kline and Mark Rothko — but that generation was simply not print-oriented. Eventually Tyler persuaded de Kooning to draw some plates for him in his Long Island Studio, but his 'point of attack' was wrong. The artist could not conceive a layered image and the coloured proofs Tyler printed for him at Gemini were not a success. Once Rauschenberg had been to Gemini, however, his contemporaries — Jasper Johns, Roy Lichtenstein, Frank Stella and Claes Oldenburg — followed.

JASPER JOHNS

plates 30-31

Like Rauschenberg, Johns had already drawn many lithographs before he arrived at Gemini. These included the 1964 *Ale cans* and the sensational *Two maps* of 1966. Three other prints Johns had made at U.L.A.E. utilized a technique in which several inks were merged together on the roller at the printing stage — a strategy known as spectrum rolling if rainbow colours are used and a common feature of nineteenth-century commercial printing. The small-scale colour-blended prints from U.L.A.E. were to be eclipsed by the ambitious large-scale project Johns undertook at Gemini when he had one set of black and grey and another set of coloured numerals printed from the same matrices. Measuring over three feet, these most literal and pragmatic stencil numbers were over twice the height of the famous U.L.A.E. *0–9* portfolios of 1960–63. To create the colour blends that Johns wanted on that scale, Tyler had to have a special automatic inking machine made. Johns' cataloguer, R. S. Field, described the prints as 'bench-marks in the history of lithographic expression', and spoke of the monochrome set as 'the most beautiful images of the Arabic numerals ever created'.[1] Joseph Young described the results as 'unparalleled in the history of lithography'.[2]

The artist once explained that he preferred ready-made subjects because they permitted him to lavish all his invention in the area of technique. He applied his entire drawing repertoire to the numerals he made at Gemini, 'trying to make each one different from the other'.[3] He put wash down with both brush and roller and used it as background over the stark 'unartful' *Figure 9*, the outline of which was reserved by a gum resist to print as a white. Like his earlier *Coat hanger*, the *Figure 6* almost disappeared under a rain of crayon strokes. The *Figure 7* included an iron-on decal

30 Jasper Johns with proofs from his *Black numeral series* of lithographs in 1968

31 Jasper Johns: *Figure 3* from the *Color numeral series*, 1968/69, 38 x 31 in (96.5 x 78.7 cm), lithograph, edition 40

32 Jasper Johns: *Figure 7* from the *Color numeral series*, 1968/69, 38 x 31 in (96.5 x 78.7 cm), lithograph, edition 40

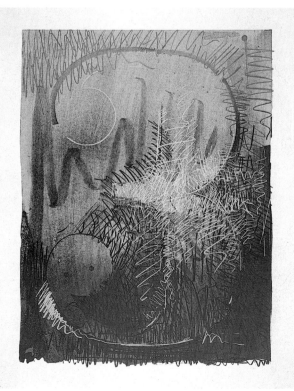

of the Mona Lisa, while a newsprint background was added to the coloured *Figure 1*   plate 32
by screenprinting a text onto the stone.

The printer, Charly Ritt, who worked on the series, was impressed by the way
Johns superimposed his extraordinary washes on stone: 'You could see down into
them like they were water . . . they were really magical'.[4] The work became an essay
in interrelated sequences, for not only were the same stones and plates used to print
the numerals 0 to 9 in monochrome and then again in colour, but the rainbow set
followed a pseudo-systematic rotation of primary and secondary colours, making another sequence within it.

In 1969, after he had completed the *Color numerals*, Johns told Joseph Young that
his impulse to make prints sprang not from a belief that it was a good way to express
himself, but from his interest in the possibility of technical innovation. Despite his long
association with U.L.A.E., he had gone to Gemini, he said, 'to see what another
printing situation was like' and what effect it would have on his work. Because of the
speed with which Tyler's many printers met his needs, he found that greater spontaneity was indeed possible. He also found, despite the fact that Gemini was a much
larger operation than U.L.A.E., that 'one's contact with the printers . . . is rather close.
It's not as impersonal as one would think'.[5]

Ken Tyler had a huge admiration for the artist's skill and found printing for him taxing
but rewarding:

> The ranges of tonality that a Johns drawn stone gets is incredible; and these are not
> reworked at all, so that you have a fresh quality about his work . . . Let's face it, he's one
> of the greatest lithographers of all time, and he is, therefore, one of the hardest to print for
> because he incorporates so many subtleties in his prints . . . his stones yield the last ounce
> of blood lithography has to yield . . .[6]

During his first visit to Gemini, Johns also drew *Gray alphabets*, which in 1968 was,   plate 33
at five feet, the biggest print he had ever made. Taking the form of an all-over tess-
ellation composed of lower case letters, the print began with a series of rubber
typeface imprints which Johns then deftly elaborated with delicate pools of wash. The
work was printed in four soft shades of grey, with two exquisite single colour cancellation proofs, one of them inscribed by the artist 'for Ken'. The print followed earlier
unique works, but nearly all Johns' graphic work has dealt with the effect that different
materials and treatments exert on essentially similar subject matter. This makes particularly inane the *New York Times* criticism at the time of *Technics and Creativity* that
the artist was making 'reproductions'.

The other major project that Johns undertook before the Museum of Modern Art
exhibition was the series of editioned *Lead reliefs* related to his inkless embossings.
Neutral grey is one of the most important ingredients in Johns' pictorial repertoire and
he liked the varied nuances the lead surface acquired through oxidation. Except for
the *Flag* which was made from the plaster cast of an earlier work in Sculpmetal, Johns
specially created the models for the reliefs in wax. Then 'female' and 'male' moulds
were used in an industrial forming machine to emboss a thin sheet of lead later ad-
hered to a rigid moulded polystyrene backing. The subjects of the reliefs included a
boy's joke shoe with a mirror inset in the toe for looking up girls' dresses, a light bulb,   plate 35
superimposed numerals, bread (with an edition of fictive slices hand-painted by the   plate 34
artist), and a toothbrush — with a handle of tin leaf and with bristles resembling gold
crowns made by a local dentist.[7] The latter was another of Johns' sardonic works on
the theme of *The critic smiles*.   plate 36

Undoubtedly both superficial as well as more penetrating commentators were able
to discern differences between the artist's east coast and west coast work, but not
all were necessarily critical. Joseph Young, for example, felt that the Gemini prints
functioned 'as a bridge from lithography's nineteenth-century autographic handcrafted approach to the more impersonal technical expression of our own time'.[8]
Clinton Adams pointed out that much of the difference in character came from different

33 Jasper Johns: *Gray alphabets*, 1968, 60 x 42 in (152.4 x 106.6 cm), lithograph, edition 59

34 Jasper Johns working on the wax model for *Numerals* from the *Lead relief series*, 1969

tools and materials. Tanya Grosman, he said, liked to work with special papers, whereas Tyler at that time used standard sheets of Arches and Rives; the large roller needed for Johns' blended numbers was very different from the more usual small composition roller. Adams recognized that '. . . things of this sort cause a shift in character . . . Maybe Johns was equally happy. Maybe this is exactly what he wanted . . .'[9]

There is also no doubt that the differences between the personalities and technical orientation of Ken Tyler and Tanya Grosman, and the contrast between bright, sunny Los Angeles and the more atmospheric Long Island had their inevitable effect on the work Johns produced. However, when someone once apologized to the artist because it was raining in Los Angeles, he said there was no need to worry as grey was his favourite colour.

The evaluation of the differences between U.L.A.E. and Gemini was more often determined by a romantic view of the artist and of what lithography had traditionally achieved, than by considering the likelihood that Johns was deliberately playing upon the different situations and utilizing them for his work. As Ken Tyler pointed out in response to the frequently made accusation that he imposed his 'Californian fetish finish' on artists:

> . . . when Jasper said: 'Now take that beautiful, beautiful wash that you've just done a marvelous job on Ken and put this grey transparent flat over it and lose fifty percent of it', we did that. Now is that the flat California look? But Jasper wanted it. It wasn't Ken Tyler telling Jasper to do it, it was because ten percent of the surface worked on with liquid tusche didn't have enough grease to survive the process. So instead of having that wonderful velvety quality across the whole surface, Johns says 'Let's put a gray flat down there . . .'[10]

Indeed Johns, whose attitude to the creative process is basically unromantic, is on record as saying that he had 'never wanted a seductive quality', whatever the medium, and had always considered himself 'a very literal artist'.[11] The assumption that a

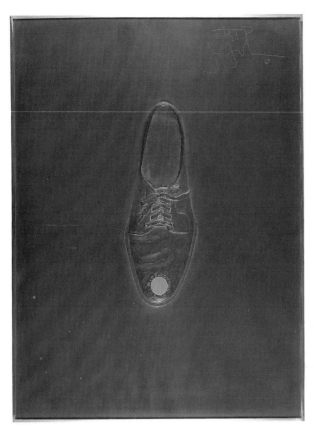

35 Jasper Johns: *High school days* from the *Lead relief series*, 1969/70, 23 x 17 in (58.4 x 43.1 cm), sheet lead, mirror, edition 60

36 Jasper Johns: *The critic smiles* from the *Lead relief series*, 1969/70, 23 x 17 in (58.4 x 43.1 cm), sheet lead, gold cast, tin leaf, edition 60

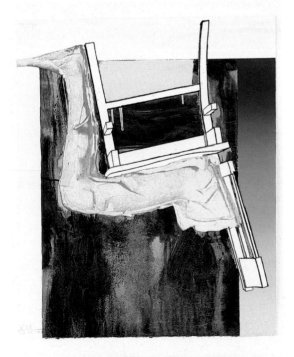

37 Jasper Johns: *Leg and chair* from *Fragments – according to what*, 1971, 35 x 30 in (88.9 x 76.2 cm), lithograph, edition 68

38 Jasper Johns: *Bent blue (second state)* from *Fragments – according to what*, 1971, 25½ x 28¼ (64.7 x 71.7 cm), lithograph with unique monotype from newspaper on each print, edition 66

39 Jasper Johns: *Fool's house*, (black state), 1972, 44 x 29 in (111.6 x 73.6 cm) lithograph, edition 67

40 Jasper Johns: *Good time Charley*, 1972, 44 x 29 in (111.6 x 73.6 cm), lithograph, edition 69

painter of such phenomenal ability would have been in the grip of events rather than determining them seems quite unsupportable. For while collaborative printing has increasingly become a case of aesthetic and technical contributions by two different intellects, the artist, as Ken Tyler pointed out:

> . . . has all the aesthetic control; we have all the technical control. The distinction gets very gray at times. There's nothing I'll say no to, but you have to learn that if the artist doesn't like something, he can say no.[12]

Indeed, Johns did say no to the first print he made at Gemini; the workshop was testing alabaster as a substitute for limestone and Johns took part in the experiment, which failed to give adequate results.

Although three-quarters of the lithographs Johns created between 1960 and 1970 were made with Tanya Grosman, only one-ninth of the prints he made over the next seven years (catalogued by Field in a separate volume[13]) were made in West Islip; more and more, the artist worked elsewhere. While the majority of prints made on Long Island gave evidence of the 'warm and slightly malerisch artistry of Tanya Grosman's workshop', an increasing proportion displayed, in Field's opinion, 'something of the intellectualization pursued at Gemini'.[14]

During the 1970s, Johns continued to explore the relativity of seeing and 'the nature of reality and its legion of surrogates', but both paintings and prints were marked by increasing sophistication and complexity. To a body of work already ironic and paradoxical, Johns added tougher concepts deriving from a study of the painter Marcel Duchamp and the philosopher Ludwig Wittgenstein and he became more difficult, introspective and hermetic.

Field has suggested that Johns often attempted to elucidate his rather obscure and difficult paintings by re-presenting aspects of them in series of prints. Six aspects of the painted polyptych *According to what*, which amounts to a lexicon of pictorial conventions, appear in the Gemini lithographic suite *Fragments — according to what*.   plate 37
The prints reveal the fact that they are details from other works in the way the images bleed off the paper. The title of the painting came from a passage in one of the artist's notebooks — 'somewhere there is a question of seeing clearly, seeing what, according to what'. *Bent blue* is perhaps the most beautiful of the six sheets; it expresses   plate 38
a concept that would have had no real meaning unless Johns had formed the word 'blue' sculpturally and had actually bent it for his painting. The print plays off extremely sensuous washes (which leave no doubt in the mind about Gemini's capabilities in this area) against more machine-like near-metallic blends from grey to grey-violet, perhaps influenced by the strange surfaces of the lead reliefs.

Field felt that few works 'achieve such a high order of integration of image, style and technique' and that 'under Ken Tyler, precision and control were never better served', yet the suite was coolly received. This indicated to Field that Johns, with his self-imposed principle of moving on and forcing change, had indeed 'managed to break out of the mold of public expectations'.[15]

In 1972, the year before Tyler left Los Angeles, Johns made a further set of lithographs at Gemini. The prints related closely to some difficult self-referential paintings executed between 1961 and 1964 — *Souvenir*, *'M'*, *Evion*, *Device*, *Zone*, *Fool's house*, *Goodtime Charley*, and *Viola*. Michael Crichton found the artist's paintings from   plates 39-40
this period 'precariously resistant to interpretation'.[16] Their rather literal lithographic re-presentation, in both coloured and black states, may reflect Johns' desire to offer the subject matter a second time without too radical a transformation. Nevertheless, the surfaces of the prints, particularly the black variants, are extremely beautiful. Field, however, felt that the artist's highly intellectual solutions actually drew the viewer's attention away from the sensuous qualities of what he did at Gemini and cautioned those 'who make qualitative judgements about the character of a publisher's production before they consider the numerous variables and intentions involved . . .'[17]

POP ARTISTS

Nevertheless, much of the work done at Gemini did reinforce Gemini's reputation for an 'industrial aesthetic', however unsatisfactory the term proved when it was really explored. Ellsworth Kelly, for whom a whiter than white paper was developed, made a whole series of abstract colour shapes placed on this stark field in active and restless formats. The prints, although perfectly flat, exploited visual paradox by suggesting a third dimension. Like Albers' work, these immaculate conceptions required meticulous workmanship.

Judith Goldman said of Roy Lichtenstein that he and Gemini 'were made for each other'.[1] In 1961, the artist was painting in an abstract expressionist style based on that of Willem de Kooning. He made the transition to Pop Art in response to a challenge from one of his sons, who bet him he couldn't paint anything as good as the Mickey Mouse in his comic book. In basing his style on commercial printing, Lichtenstein even adopted Ben Day dots, a form of mechanical tinting which creates an illusion of pink from a single printing of red, so as to get the maximum effect from the minimum number of passages through the press. While at first sight Lichtenstein's works give an impression of being blindly copied, in fact the banal images lifted from comic strips were subtly edited as Lichtenstein composed them into large-scale paintings. Nevertheless, the New York art world was initially horrified by this brash and blatant development, although this new style, with its use of subject matter from the consumer society, eventually brought an expanded audience to the enjoyment of art.

Lichtenstein told an interviewer in 1963 that he was 'anti-contemplative, anti-nuance, anti-getting-away-from-the-tyranny of the rectangle, anti-movement and -light, anti-mystery, anti-paint-quality, anti-Zen . . .'[2] He added that although everybody called Pop Art 'American painting', it was in fact industrial painting, for it employed the techniques of mass-production, including a smooth and impersonal handling of surface that tried to hide the record of the hand.[3]

Lichtenstein told Joseph Young, tongue-in-cheek, that he had come to Gemini in January 1969 because 'there are very few places where you can make a mark and have fifteen people work on it!'. He also revealed that he processed both paintings and prints in roughly similar ways, using dot stencils and a step by step method. As Young commented:

> . . . [it] makes one wonder if his prints are not aesthetically superior to his paintings, since the prints, by appearing to have been mechanically produced, seem to better approximate the impersonal look which the artist strives to attain.[4]

Much of Lichtenstein's work was based on paintings by famous artists. Two of his suites at Gemini brilliantly utilized the serial imagery made possible through the rotation of stencils, taking as a point of departure the dawn-to-dusk sequences of haystacks and cathedrals painted by the Impressionist artist, Claude Monet, towards the end of the nineteenth century. For the prints based on Rouen Cathedral, the printers actually used Lichtenstein's painting stencils, corrected so as to be more systematic and mechanical. The 'manufactured Monets', a form of 'quick cheap Impressionism',[5] even exhibited similar characteristics to the paintings of the French artist by dissolving at close quarters and coming into focus at a distance.

plate 41
plate 42

The prints are also wonderfully economical in their use of colour. Yellow on white suggests the intensity of sunlight, black on blue conveys the gloom of midnight, while blue and red, singly or combined, suggest intermediate times of day. Some of the prints look as if they have been overprinted with a grid, when what one actually sees is the white of the unprinted paper. Others throb and flash with dazzling optical pat-

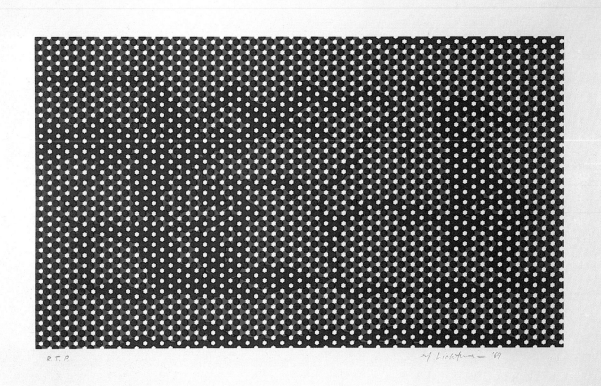

R.T.P.   ◦f Lichten— '69

41 Roy Lichtenstein: *Haystack 4*, 1969, 20½ x 30¾ in (52.0 x 78.1 cm), lithograph, screenprint, edition 100

42 Roy Lichtenstein: *Cathedral 5*, 1969, 48½ x 32½ in (123.1 x 82.5 cm), lithograph, screenprint, edition 75

43 Roy Lichtenstein: *Peace through chemistry II*, 1970, 37¼ x 63 in (94.6 x 160.0 cm), lithograph, screenprint, edition 43

44 Roy Lichtenstein: *Peace through chemistry bronze*, 1970, 27¼ x 46¼ x 1¼ in (69.2 x 117.4 x 3.1 cm), cast bronze relief, edition 38

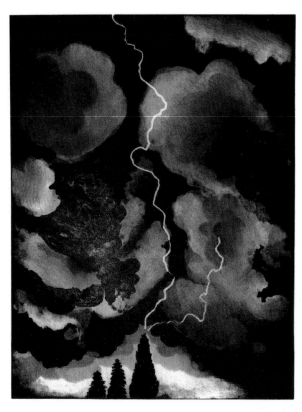

terns of rosettes and stars, made by portions of the sheet glimpsed between the superimposed dots. The suites were primarily lithographic, but Tyler, who as time went on became more and more involved in mixed-media prints, did not hesitate to utilize screenprinting where necessary and completed the smaller scale *Haystacks* with an embossed black from a line block. It was an important part of Tyler's credo that processes should not be separated into hermetic compartments and he again combined three techniques for Lichtenstein's witty adaptation, in his *Bull profile series*, of the theme of a Picasso lithograph in which a bull mutates from the schematic to the abstract.

When Lichtenstein returned to Gemini the following year, he developed works based on another of his art historical concerns — the 'art moderne' or 'art deco' of the 1930s. The artist was fascinated by the style's optimism, which was maintained even during the Depression, and by the feeling 'that man could work with the machine to obtain a better living and a great future'. He liked the naive idea of modernity, the 'Platonism of the production line'. *Peace through chemistry* is an imaginary mural that might have been painted by an American artist working for the federal relief agency set up during the period of severe unemployment. Lichtenstein thought of the imagery as 'absolutely useless Cubism . . . a play on supercomposition as it might be learned in school . . .' and he exclaimed of the title: 'What an unlikely notion!'.[6]

Some of the versions of the print maintained Tyler's interest in large scale and measured over five feet across. There was also a bronze relief turned out by a firm making commemorative plaques for Disneyland. In addition, Lichtenstein explored, through various prints and multiples, the theme of the modern head. These works, which also parody the 1930s, were stimulated by a group of Jawlensky's Constructivist heads that Lichtenstein saw at the Pasadena Art Museum in 1968. Based on drawings and cardboard maquettes with other forms in plaster and wood, various three-dimensional prototypes were considered — black enamel over aluminium and glass, for example. In the end, the editions were produced in brass and walnut wood. Of five experimental printed head forms, one was a woodcut, unusual

45 David Hockney: *Study of lightning*, 1973, 30 x 22 (76.2 x 55.8 cm), lithograph, edition 60

46 David Hockney: *Ten palm trees in mist*, 1973, 36 x 29 (91.4 x 73.6 cm), lithograph, edition 8

plate 43

plate 44

47 David Hockney: *Snow without colour*, 1973, 42 x 33 in (106.6 x 83.8 cm), lithograph, screenprint, edition 38

48   David Hockney: *Mist* from the *Weather series*, 1973, 37 x 32 in (93.9 x 81.2 cm), lithograph, edition 98

49   David Hockney: *Rain* from the *Weather series*, 1973, 39 x 31½ in (99.6 x 80.0 cm), lithograph, screenprint, edition 98

50   David Hockney: *Wind* from the *Weather series*, 1973, 40 x 31 in (101.6 x 78.7 cm), lithograph, screenprint, edition 98

O.K to pull.

davis hockney 73

51 David Hockney: *Sun* from the *Weather series*, 1973, 37¼ x 30½ in (94.6 x 77.4 cm), lithograph, screenprint, edition 98

for its time, its dots cut by an automatic router. Two prints were made from zinc cuts, which are photomechanical relief blocks without half-tone dots. Another was made of engraved anodized and printed aluminium and the fourth from embossed graphite with a die-cut paper overlay.

In 1973, the year Tyler left the west coast, David Hockney returned to Gemini for a sustained period of work. Although he is often spoken of as a Pop artist, Hockney is actually a traditional draughtsman who sets down his wonderful portraits of friends directly onto the plate or stone, often using the print workshop as a branch of his studio. As the years have passed, his drawings have been simplified to a few evocative brush lines of great confidence and freedom, in contrast to the almost nineteenth-century crayon techniques he adopted when he began making lithographs at Gemini. Nevertheless, it would be difficult for him to improve on the exquisite *Celia smoking*, in which his friend is wreathed in the tenuous wisps issuing from her cigarette. During the same period, Hockney drew a portrait entitled *The master printer of Los Angeles*, in which he shows Tyler sitting in front of a print from the artist's *Weather series*.

Hockney used to leave Britain for southern California for part of each year. The *Weather series* celebrates the west coast sunshine, mist exquisitely enveloping a row of palm trees, puddles of rain, a shaft of lightning recalling Hogarth, a snow scene straight out of Japanese Ukiyo-e woodblock prints and a humorous evocation of *Wind*, in which four of the artist's own prints blow away down Melrose Avenue, where the Gemini workshop was situated. plates 48-51

CLAES OLDENBURG AND THE MULTIPLE

The three-dimensional art form known as the multiple became more and more characteristic of Gemini's work as the 1960s progressed. Rosa Esman of Tanglewood Editions and Marian Goodman of Multiples Inc. were among the first to produce this kind of art object in America, but the concept had first taken root in Europe as a by-product of closer ties between art and technology. The most idealistic multiples utilized mass-production techniques for unlimited editions, so as to extend opportunities for art ownership to the impecunious. They were fundamentally different from traditional sculptures cast in limited numbers for an élite. Some commentators, among them Janet Daley, found the very notion of the multiple philistine and corrupting because of the taint of commercialism and the fact that mass-production entailed appealing to the lowest common denominator of taste.[1] Others were more optimistic. Karl Gerstner of édition MAT,[2] founded in 1959, tried to make available works of high quality which although produced in editions of one hundred left an individual element to be contributed by each owner. The Jasper Johns multiple that Gemini made to be distributed with the *Technics and Creativity* catalogue was of this order, in that Johns provided a simply drawn but uncoloured target, a brush, a palette of the three primary colours, and, beside his signature, a space where the collaborating owner could also sign. Hilton Kramer, beside himself, devoted several column inches of the *New York Times* to a withering condemnation of this 'Jasper Johns coloring book'.[3]

One of the most intelligent articles about the whole mid-sixties phenomenon was written by the British art historian Reyner Banham, who pointed out that when a famous artist talked a big industrialist into taking him on 'as something between a domestic pet and a promotional gimmick', the product was usually a one-off prestige job. Rather than link up with industrial giants, Banham argued, artists could obtain the service they needed from cottage industries such as 'Fred Bloggs (Plastics) 1964 Ltd. of the Balls Pond Road', listed in the yellow pages.[4] In the same way, Pontus Hultén, looking at the effect of the machine on art, found that the high degree of polish necessary invariably had to be obtained by hand, so that most art aspiring to a machine aesthetic was actually expensive, specialized and handmade.[5]

Because of its location amidst the aircraft, aerospace, film and scientific engineering industries, when it came to multiples, Gemini was ideally placed to find small firms able to produce almost anything artists wanted. In his role as go-between, Tyler, ably supported by his partners, became an entrepreneur interpreting artists' intentions to manufacturers. These intentions were frequently out-of-the-ordinary, and even in Hollywood there must have been some raised eyebrows at Claes Oldenburg's specification for an ice bag, measuring eighteen feet in diameter, and able to swivel and breathe heavily!

Although it was far easier to make a profit on straightforward lithographic editions and Tyler later said in a panel discussion that he couldn't think of one multiple where 'he came out ahead',[6] it was nevertheless Gemini's policy to encourage technological advance through research-oriented collaboration. Tyler told a reporter that once his firm knew what an artist wanted, it might do up to a year's independent investigation before collaborating with an appropriate company from its 'who's who of California industry'. The printer explained to Joseph Young that any great artist could produce a beautiful drawing to be made into a lithograph; this was no real challenge. Gemini wanted to increase the dimensions of printmaking by pushing the media as far as they

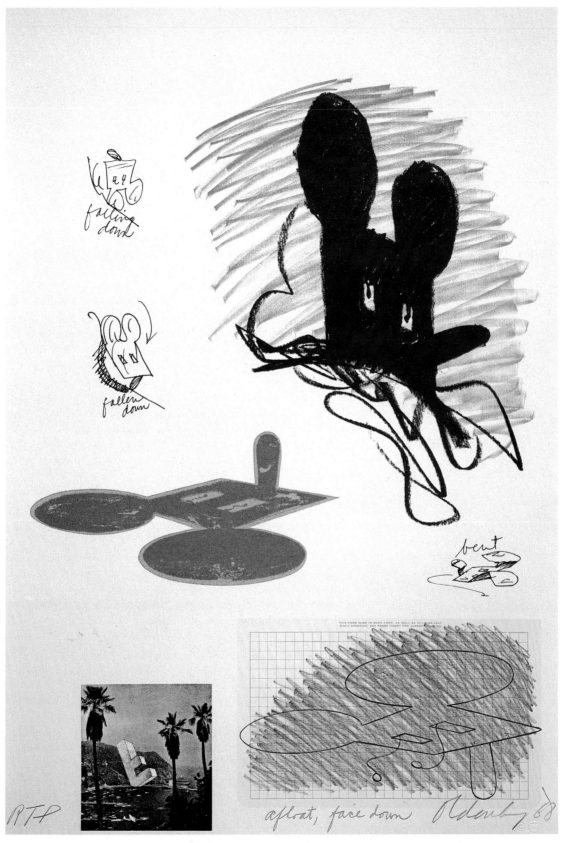

52 Claes Oldenburg, *Notes (Geometrical mouse as hilltop, city park and floating sculptures)*, 1968, 22¾ x 15¾ (57.8 x 40.0 cm), lithograph, edition 100

could go. As Tyler put it: 'we keep a three-ring circus going'[7]; this became more and more true as the 1960s proceeded.

Gemini entered into its most extensive three-dimensional projects for the sculptor Claes Oldenburg, beginning with a relief and then moving to free-standing and kinetic sculptures.

Oldenburg had come to the notice of the art world in 1961 when he created his environmental work known as 'The Store', for which he modelled food and other kinds of merchandise in muslin and plaster. By 1962, he was making soft, large-scale

53 Claes Oldenburg, *Notes (Kneeling building, Gemini chop and skate monument)*, 1968, 22¾ x 15¾ in (57.8 x 40.0 cm), lithograph, edition 100

54 Gemini G.E.L.'s press room during the proofing of Rauschenberg's *Stoned moon* project, September 1969

objects such as foam rubber hamburgers, fake leopard skin good humour bars, and fried potatoes of calico with vinyl ketchup. Then he began to formulate grandiose plans for huge-scale monuments based on unlikely human body parts or on inanimate objects not normally thought of as fitting subjects for sculpture — for example, lipsticks and cigarette butts. Unlike most Pop artists, Oldenburg was fascinated by the idea of surreal metamorphosis, through which an object could suggest something quite different, particularly if made in soft materials. He made considerable play with the erotic implications of these strategies.

Oldenburg was ideally suited to the concept of multiples, and, by the time he went to Gemini, he had already made several for other publishers. They included a fibreglass potato hand-painted on an assembly line, a screenprinted felt teabag with rayon cord trapped inside a plastic carapace and, inspired in swinging London by the area of leg between the top of the knee-boot and the bottom of the mini-skirt, a pair of squeezable latex knees. These were about as sensual as a cold hot-water bottle, but they satisfied Oldenburg in his obsession for objects that looked hard but were actually pliant.

Although he had made a few prints before going to Gemini, Oldenburg had not really taken to printmaking. The deal Tyler made with him was that if he felt the project wasn't working, he could just walk away. Oldenburg later told an interviewer that, while he liked to circulate his ideas and was fascinated by multiplicity, he disliked lithography because he preferred to draw on a flexible receptive medium such as 'a nice strong piece of white paper that I can erase'. He was also more at home in intimate conditions and felt uneasy 'stepping on stage . . . doing something in front of everybody'. Because of the adjustments necessary, he found printmaking 'an excruciatingly unpleasant activity like going to the hospital for an operation'.[8]

Tyler did everything he could to try and make Oldenburg comfortable in the Gemini workshop. As it was the sculptor's practice to keep a constant note of his ideas, filling perhaps six hundred sheets a year with drawings and collages, Tyler designed a paper holder and gave him a special ball-point pen filled with lithographic ink so that his sketches could be captured in all their doodled spontaneity.

The resulting twelve lithographs of *Notes*, published in 1968, are an on-the-spot plates 52-53

plate 54

record of Oldenburg's encounters as he worked at Gemini and moved about Los Angeles. The shape of the ink 'draw-downs' made to test colour in the lithography studio suggested edifices made of dropped ice cream cones. Some of the more intimate parts of the anatomy of Kay Tyler's huge Afghan hound found themselves transformed into a fantastic monument. Oldenburg could make endless bizarre connections between visual stimuli; when his hotel served his breakfast tea in the morning, supplying two sugar cubes in a paper cup, the image reminded the artist of the two front teeth of the girl on the desk at Gemini, which in turn suggested the workshop's embossed printer's chop. A nose in *Notes* became a freeway tunnel entrance and then developed into an incredibly funky multiple called *Double-nose/purse/ punching bag/ashtray*, which took a dozen collaborators to produce. The printing of *Notes* entailed 104 colours and 112 press runs, including embossing. The proof copy at the Australian National Gallery is inscribed by the artist: 'To Ken, with greatest affection for a heroic job!'.

plate 52

Other long-standing obsessions of the artist were also recorded, for example his geometric Mickey Mouse, the head of which, with circular ears, protruding tongue and rectangular face with shuttered eyes, had been suggested by the form of early film cameras. Oldenburg had used the mouse head as a performance mask as well as proposing it as the façade for a contemporary art museum in Chicago. Now, in *Notes*, he visualized it as a hilltop sculpture, a city park, or floating on a pond like a lily pad. In 1969, a unique sculpture of the mouse, with ears measuring six feet, had been shown in Oldenburg's retrospective at the Museum of Modern Art. A year later Gemini recreated it as a multiple with a nine-inch ear, made in aluminium with an anodized matte finish. The shop also produced an unlimited edition die-cut paper version with six-inch ears to retail at twenty dollars, thereby fulfilling a multiple's most democratic

plate 55

purpose. By 1972, Oldenburg had caused about five thousand mice to come into being; as a sculptor interested in largeness, he relished the idea of quantity as a kind of scale.

The first multiple he made at Gemini, however, was the one which caused the most anguish, even though the later *Icebag* outstripped it in complexity. As a child, the sculptor had been fascinated by a maroon model of the 1936 streamlined Chrysler Airflow car with headlights, and he later became friendly with the son of the man who

55 Claes Oldenburg: *Geometric mice, scale C and scale D*, 1971, 9 and 6 in. ear (22.8 and 15.2 cm ear), anodized black aluminium and printed card respectively, editions 120 and unlimited

designed it. Intrigued by cars as the machines closest to man, Oldenburg wanted to make a model of the Airflow in a translucent material that, like his latex knees, would be firm but appear soft and, although rigid, would be flexible enough to give if pressed. plate 57 He spent a year on the wooden relief from which the moulds for the edition were produced and drew a lithograph over which the translucent cast was to be mounted. In her analysis of what Tyler later called an object print, the art historian Barbara Rose linked Oldenburg's car with the strange nature-machine imagined by the Futurist poet Marinetti, who had thought the racing automobile more beautiful than classical sculpture. Barbara Rose also suggested that the lido-coloured *Airflow* was an essay in style, fusing an underlying personal expressionist subjective drawing with the impersonal mechanical geometry of the car's outer skin.[9]

As vacuum forming could not produce the depth Oldenburg wanted, Tyler engaged in endless experiments with vinyls, polyesters, polyurethanes, polyethylenes and silicons, producing twelve polyester models before arriving at an ideal elastometric plate 56 material. Finding a technician who specialized in plastics and who could also identify with an art project was a major undertaking, but eventually Tyler located two competent consultants. In his report to the National Endowment for the Arts, which had contributed twenty thousand dollars to Gemini for research and development, Tyler estimated that by the time it was completed the project would have cost one hundred thousand dollars. He also observed, as Reyner Banham had done before him, that whereas Gemini was searching for a means to make high quality limited editions, industry was basically engaged in a search for the opposite. In conclusion, he pointed out that one could have purchased a real Chrysler Airflow in the 1930s for less than it was going to cost for the Oldenburg multiple in 1969! In fact the multiple finally cost twice as much to buy as the original car.

Nor, in the end, could Gemini do anything but lose money on the project, because the first polyurethane casts discoloured and had to be recalled and replaced. As Judith Goldman later related:

> . . . while Oldenburg's art wittily mocked the industrial, Tyler ironically produced it. Tyler's relationship to Oldenburg was similar to his relationship with Albers. He was the industrial researcher who found the means to produce a swimming pool blue-green car; he was also the General Motors executive who, when the swimming pool blue-green car turned yellow, recalled the defective models and made new ones . . .[10]

Oldenburg's *Icebag* was equally demanding, but at the same time it constituted a more satisfying success story. The project arose out of Maurice Tuchman's Art and Technology programme which was devised at the Los Angeles County Museum between 1967 and 1970 to bring artists and industry together.

Oldenburg was introduced to Walt Disney Productions and hoped they would help him to mechanize some of his sculptural ideas, but Disney later backed out of the involvement. The sculptor confided to Max Kozloff years later that he had been fascinated to find out 'what people who have been making animals without genitalia for thirty years are like'.[11] For their part, Disney Productions, as a 'family-directed operation', were possibly somewhat wary of an artist who habitually endowed the most prosaic objects with sexual functions. For when Disney finally severed the connection, Oldenburg was considering a rising and falling screw exuding oil, a giant toothpaste tube raised by the emission of the paste inside it and a project which later developed into an inflatable banana. Even the *Icebag* was connected in Oldenburg's mind with breasts and stomachs, as well as (among other things) his own beret, domes, Chinese cookies, Mount Fuji and a geyser in the Yellowstone National Park; he intended it to breathe heavily while at rest.

Oldenburg had been hoping to have this kinetic *Icebag* ready in time for the Expo 70 exhibition in Osaka, for the Art and Technology artists had been invited to show their works in the U.S. Pavilion which over ten million people were expected to visit. When Disney pulled out of the scheme in the middle of 1969, Oldenberg was left with

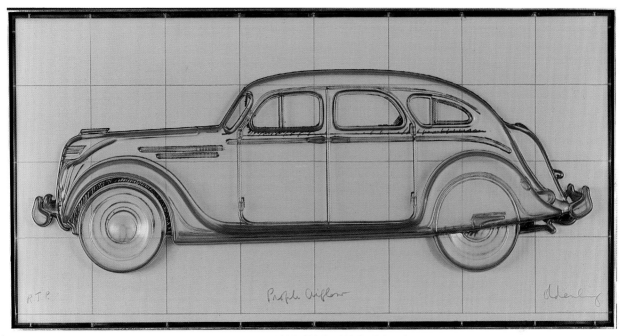

56 Claes Oldenburg: *Profile Airflow*, 1969, 35½ x 65½ x 2½ in (90.1 x 166.3 x 6.3 cm), moulded polyurethane relief over lithograph, edition 75

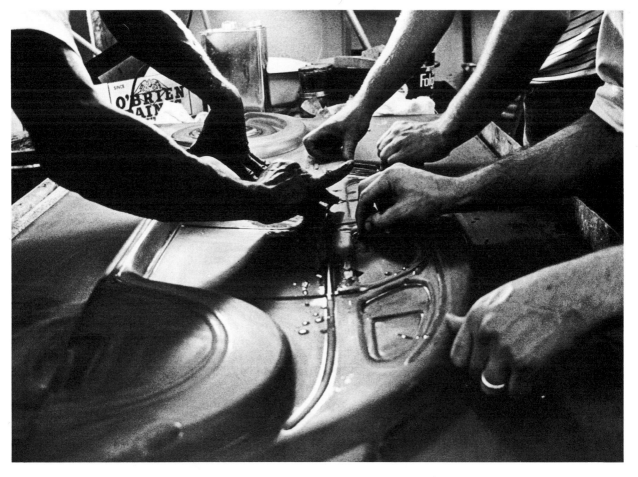

57 Wet and dry sanding of the mould for *Profile Airflow*, 1969

only a few months to complete the project, for the *Icebag* was due to leave for Japan by January 1970. After one or two abortive attempts to activate other schemes, Maurice Tuchman asked Tyler for help and Gemini came to the rescue.

From then on, the operation became a nightmare, because time and money for the project were both in such short supply. Oldenburg had originally intended his *Icebag* to measure thirty feet across, but in the end this had to be reduced to eighteen feet. Even if transportation had not presented a problem, no seamstress in the country could have sewn the elephantine amounts of pink polyvinyl required for the sculpture, which took Sid Felsen a week on the telephone to locate. According to Tyler, the seamstresses who eventually constructed the *Icebag* were positively heroic. The engineers who had custom-built presses to Tyler's specification advised on the complicated hydraulics necessary to get the movements the artist wanted. Then the Kroffts of Krofft Enterprises, who treated the *Icebag* like a character in one of their movies, signed a contract committing themselves to work until they dropped in order to complete the sculpture on time. Eventually the *Icebag* performed its complicated antics, rising from seven to sixteen feet, writhing, tilting its cap, and then settling back again for its resting period of heavy breathing. Tyler's account to Tuchman of the exertions of Gemini staff and of other collaborators was breathless and exultant, for he particularly revels in the theatrical spirit which ensures that at all costs the show will go on.[12]

Although one prototype icebag got caught in its gears 'and ate itself' during a filming session, two of smaller scale, measuring four feet and twelve feet in diameter respectively, were eventually manufactured as Gemini multiples.

As for Oldenburg, he felt that collaborating with industry necessitated many compromises and noted:

> In technology you have to be very sure what you're doing before you give the orders to go ahead, so it's an activity which in every way denies the freedom and pleasure of being an artist.[13]

Nevertheless, he was rather tickled by the idea that so much time and effort had been expended on such a foolish thing as a deep-breathing ice bag and in the end did not regret the wear and tear the effort had also cost him.

Oldenburg was not the only artist whose multiples were produced at Gemini during the 1970s, for a number of other projects proceeded simultaneously. A series of *Cubes*, made of five colour-offset lithographs sandwiched between layers of plastic, was made for Ron Davis in 1970. The following year saw the publication of John Chamberlain's *Le Molé* — a polyester resin cast with a sophisticated finish of vaporized crystals providing 'a luminescent sheen reminiscent of both Tiffany glass and the metallic paint used on automobiles in the late 1940s'.[14] For Edward Kienholz, Gemini realized *Sawdy*, a car door behind the window of which was a printed tableau of a black man being attacked for fraternizing with a white woman. The edition of fifty doors was ordered from the local Datsun dealer and the Japanese car manufacturers must have wondered what it was about Los Angeles that caused so many accidents to the same door of the same model!

By this time, Gemini had developed vast resources. It boasted three hydraulic presses of different bed sizes custom-made to Tyler's specifications, several screenprinting benches, a sculpture workshop and as many as eighteen in-house staff, plus the external collaborators. Tyler spent less and less time printing and more and more time acting as a go-between, and he began to long for the old one-to-one relationship with artists that he had previously enjoyed. Philosophical differences had also arisen between himself and his partners as to the future direction of the shop and the nature of experimental projects. In addition, his partners disagreed about opening a satellite workshop in the east and resisted the installation of an offset press, which Tyler regarded as inevitable.

FRANK STELLA AND THE OFFSET PRESS

Offset — in which an automatically inked and photomechanically made image is transferred from the metal plate to a rubber blanket and thence to paper — is today the most common quantity-production printing process. There are many types of offset press, ranging from the late nineteenth century model still used by Stanley Jones at the Curwen Studio in London to the high-speed multicolour rotary presses of modern industry, which devour huge quantities of paper in a day.

plate 5

Because of its greater mechanization and its association with commercial printing (which casts it as the enemy of humanistic values), offset has generally been frowned on as a means of making fine art, whereas its characteristics in fact give it a particular relevance to artists. It sets down a very light layer of ink in a way that facilitates the multiple superimposition of colour and renders fine detail with exquisite fidelity. Perhaps most usefully of all, it permits an original lithographic drawing (for plates do not *have* to be made photomechanically) to be set down without reversal, since unlike the direct process, the double transfer, first onto the blanket then onto the paper, ensures that the image ends up exactly as drawn. A recent catalogue for an exhibition of fine art offset prints noted that the process '. . . faced with the pervasive romance of the hand-pulled image in contrast to its own connection with commercial mass-production, was all but invisible as an artist's medium'.[1] Bill Goldston, trained to use offset in the Army, still remembers the tensions created when he suggested to Tanya Grosman that she should introduce it, although Jasper Johns, with his 1971 print *Decoy*, was instrumental in helping to break down her resistance.[2]

Despite the fact that there was no offset press at Gemini, a number of projects — those by Ron Davis and Kenneth Price, for example — utilized the services of outside offset firms. And although Gemini's small-scale crayon lithographs for an album of prints based on Frank Stella's paintings were printed direct from stones or metal plates, the paper for the black series was first tinted at Blair Lithography on an offset press.

Richard Axsom, the cataloguer of Stella's prints, claims that Stella was 'among the first artists to adapt offset lithography to fine art printing',[3] although this is not actually the case. Between the wars, for example, Lynton Kistler, the Los Angeles printer, worked brilliantly with Jean Charlot on a book in hand-drawn colour offset, while at the same time, in England, the Curwen Press was encouraging a number of important British artists to use the process. Although June Wayne felt she should focus exclusively on the revival of direct printing and did not have either room or finance for offset equipment at Tamarind, she had no objection to the process per se, having made her own *Fables* by the offset method in 1955.[4] Eugene Feldman pioneered inventive experimentation at a commercial printing establishment in Philadelphia around the same time.[5] By the beginning of the 1960s in England, Stanley Jones was editioning offset prints for Henry Moore and John Piper at the Curwen Studio,[6] while another British publisher, including Allen Jones in an extensive portfolio called *Wapping to Windsor*, made a deliberate attempt to popularize that form of printing.[7] Even S. W. Hayter, who was not particularly dedicated to lithography in any form, acknowledged in *About Prints*, published in 1962,[8] that the most commercial processes were theoretically capable of creative use and he illustrated his point with an offset print by the Swedish artist, C. O. Hultén.

plate 58

In 1972, Stella, who until that time had made all his prints with Gemini, defected to the Petersburg Press in London and used the facilities available at a commercial lithographic shop to create a number of multicolour prints related to his *Concentric square* and *Mitered maze* paintings. In a panel discussion of 1983, Tyler observed that it was '. . . always tough to think your people are leaving you for somebody else'.[9] When Stella went to London to use offset, Tyler must have experienced pangs similar to those that Tanya Grosman felt when Johns and Rauschenberg left her to work with him at Gemini.

On his return to Gemini in 1973, Stella's attitude to printmaking began to alter substantially. His earliest prints were finely crayoned lithographs showing various degrees of perceptible handling; despite the fact that some of them are registered on graph paper with exquisite precision, they were always less machine-made, slick and impersonal than people supposed. In 1973 the crayoning increased in vigour until it became positively calligraphic in quality. The large and complex screenprint *Double gray scramble* involved multi-coloured and grey scale sequences of squares within squares which required 150 runs through the press, in order to sandwich Stella's textured drawing of each band between two flat transparent layers of the same colour. Then, in *Eccentric polygons*, the last portfolio that Tyler worked on before he left Los Angeles, Stella indulged in vigorous drawing on geometric forms, the shapes of which introduced a new kind of spatial tension into his work. Their multiple overprinting with flat and transparent tones marks an additive and evolutionary rather than a preconceived approach and heralds a 'distinct change' in printmaking method. Stella explained that he had stopped making versions of his paintings, had loosened up his drawing and had adopted the traditional methods he had previously avoided because they were:

plate 54

58 Allen Jones: *Runnymede* from *Wapping to Windsor*, 1959, 19½ x 24½ in (49.5 x 62.2 cm), offset lithograph, edition 200

59 Frank Stella: *Double gray scramble*, 1973, 29 x 50¼ in (73.7 x 128.9 cm), screenprint, edition 100

. . . sort of sissy-like, it was like giving into the medium and I didn't really want to do it. I really just didn't want to be bothered. I mean I didn't see the point in it. I knew you could do beautiful things, but I could do beautiful things making paintings. I didn't need to waste my time with the prints.[10]

Although some critics saw the artist's early prints as more than reproductions of his paintings and noted the subtle dialectic between the image and the paper, Axsom observes that for the most part Stella's west coast prints were either disregarded in the critical literature, or slated. When *Technics and Creativity* was reviewed, Shirey described the artist's colourful interlaced geometries as 'more like antimacassars',[11] while Joseph Young saw Stella 'rapidly sinking into the quagmire known to the trade as "signature prints"'.[12] By 1983, however, at the end of an amazingly productive run of several years in Tyler's Bedford Village workshop, Stella, in common with everyone else, no longer believed prints were a waste of time.

TYLER ON THE EAST COAST 1974-1985

AFTER THE ECSTASY, THE LAUNDRY

The most Tyler has said about his break with his partners late in 1973 is that it was a divorce and that 'people do not talk about their divorces', but as the writer to whom he made this comment went on to observe — 'Tyler is not a man who shares space easily'.[1]

Even as early as 1971, the date of the Museum of Modern Art's *Technics and Creativity* exhibition in New York, Tyler began to feel he was ready for a change. Notwithstanding the criticism of the show, he knew that during the six years he had run Gemini his shop had produced an impressive body of work. He also had a staff that he felt was 'one of the best if not *the* best of any workshop in the world', but he perceived that Gemini was leaving the area of 'a thoughtful caring inventive cottage industry' to become a bigger more powerful organization that needed even more extensive space, staff and income to sustain it. Although he knew that he himself had helped to create that state of affairs, Tyler experienced a profound need to redirect his life, to escape from the 'showbiz' and socializing and to return to a simple one-press studio where he could 'slow down and contemplate the universe'.

> I left with that in mind. Unfortunately, the legal battle that followed forced me to begin a much larger production and shop than I wanted at that time, just to pay for everything . . . But now, in retrospect, it doesn't seem to matter as much, because I have found a more comfortable level to operate on. I function, I believe, more successfully here and I think my work has improved.
> Ironically, the flak that the Museum of Modern Art show received actually helped me and freed me from a situation that had run its course.[2]

Although to the casual observer Tyler's confidence appears unbounded, in fact he was bruised and cut up by the hostility towards Gemini and did not immediately see that it might help him to formulate a new approach.

> At the time that it's happening, you're pretty crushed. You can get ticked off very easily because you're in a very emotional business. I think it's an emotional business. I get very involved in my work . . . I put everything I've got into what I'm doing . . .[3]

Judith Goldman considers that the fusillade of criticism directed at *Technics and Creativity* was in part a snobbish gesture against what the east perceived as west coast tinsel, but was chiefly a reaction to the workshop's industrial aesthetic, which was 'ahead of its time'. She felt the sheer size of Tyler's lithographs, to which traditional standards of connoisseurship could not be applied, 'upset the existing order in the graphic arts'.[4] As the journalist Mark Rosin expressed it in *Harper's Bazaar*: 'Gemini is suspect to all those who believe that artists must live in squalor, that tech-

60 Ken Tyler at one of his presses during the proofing of *Lament for Lorca* in 1982

nology kills humanity, that old is beautiful and that any work of art which is not unique is mass-produced'.[5]

Whichever way one interprets events, Tyler, borrowing a Zen saying, comments: 'after the ecstasy, the laundry'. During the inevitable stock-taking in the altering climate of the early 1970s, his ideas underwent considerable change.

Quite apart from Tyler's change of heart, *frisson* is now built in to the operation of the art market where, ironically, the pressure for stylistic novelty induces a kind of conformity. Pontus Hultén, in his catalogue *The Machine*, describes the New York art world as a place where movements are expected to follow each other like fashions:

> . . . such mechanization of art history is all the more unnecessary because it is totally unproductive and arises out of laziness and a lack of imagination . . . Free expressions . . . are forced into an artificial pattern of development, because it is easier to present them in that way . . . Art is viewed as a consumer product and sold on that basis; therefore at the opening of every season a new model must be unveiled . . .[6]

In answer to this cyclical need for change and variation, such movement as there had been towards the machine began to swing conservatively back towards the hand, a tendency exacerbated by the economic down-turn occasioned by the oil crisis. Fear of running out of fossil fuels, an ever-increasing awareness of the many ecological issues at stake and a shortage of the by-products of oil (which made itself felt in the price and availability of materials for fine art printing), all contributed to the anti-technological mood. The relief experienced by curators at the return to traditional standards of connoisseurship was both transparent and sustained. Robert Flynn Johnson, curator of the Achenbach Foundation at the Fine Arts Museums, San Francisco, said in 1978:

> I am personally most pleased that we are starting to get away from . . . the multiple print that is run out in 100 or 200 impressions, each one of which is pristine and all that. I prefer the idea of the artist's touch.[7]

Similarly, in his summary of recent American print history, the curator Barry Walker wrote: '. . . one of the most interesting and encouraging phenomena of the last few years is the reaction against the 'cool' print, the perfect unvarying edition that shows no trace of the artist's hand'.[8]

Irwin Hollander, the Tamarind-trained master printer who ran a shop in New York until 1972, also confessed that after a while perfection had become boring, while his wife, Deanna, expressed a desire for 'a printer's smudge, a little bit off register, to give us something back to where the human is'.[9]

While some artists reacted like seismographs, immediately adjusting their orientation, the more resolute, like Albers (who once again christened Tyler's new shop), remained unmoved. As time progressed and conceptual artists offered their own critique of the situation, critics and art historians, observing a greater range of aesthetic options than had ever been seen before, began to discuss whether perhaps the new plurality had actually destroyed the concept of an avant-garde.

In printmaking, the impetus for change caused techniques which had been partially eclipsed to be resuscitated. A new approach to etching — pioneered since the early 1960s by Kathan Brown of Crown Point Press and supported during the 1970s by the remarkable publisher Robert Feldman of Parasol — became a popular alternative to lithography. While the Atelier 17 etching style had survived in the colleges as the most popular method for printmakers doing all their own work, a body of collaborative intaglio printers now emerged to service the needs of leading painters. One of the quite distinct features of this new trend was the acceptance and absolute mastery of aquatint, which Hayter had largely eschewed because 'it destroys line and drives out light'.[10] Just as the skill necessary for printing flat lithographic colour had been scientifically mastered during the 1960s, so now in the 1970s, when texture was again demanded, the discipline was developed to print the equally difficult pure, even areas of aquatint for minimalists.

A speedy reaction to minimalism, in the guise of a revivified form of expressionism, focused attention again on the vigour and simplicity of the woodcut. Monotypes — a cross between prints and drawings which do not entail editioning and which exist in one or at the most two impressions — came into vogue, and the New York Metropolitan Museum's monotype exhibition at the end of the decade aroused considerable interest. Publishers wanting to force a new approach began to actively resist the multiplicity and allegedly machine-like qualities of the art of the 1960s. In 1972, the New York dealer Brooke Alexander, having grown tired of the even surface that prevailed in American lithography',[11] invited twenty-six artists to combine traditional graphic media with hand-colouring to create a work that would fall somewhere between a drawing and a print, between uniqueness and ubiquity.

In certain essential areas — in his commitment to research and development, in his insistent belief that the artist should be free of limitations and in what has been called his 'ambition and peripatetic inventiveness'[12] — Tyler himself remained unchanged. As a professional serving the needs of artists engaged in making prints, however, he had both to react to new developments and to help initiate them. At his new shop, Tyler Graphics, in Bedford Village, there was far less of the west coast talk about the challenge and excitement of replicating large editions identically, and there was a corresponding absence of proselytism for the erosion of barriers between art and technology. Moreover, although many 'stars' who had known Tyler at Gemini also worked with him in the east, he now introduced to printmaking a number of artists who were not quite such household names. While Gemini had been mostly a man's world, printing only for Josef Albers' wife Anni, the climate at Bedford Village grew daily more sympathetic to women. Tyler began to work with Helen Frankenthaler, Joan Mitchell and Nancy Graves, and he took on a woman intaglio printer, Betty Fiske, who printed some 'marvelous etchings'.[13]

plate 86
plate 61

Some of the editions produced at the new shop were extensive and still displayed the characteristic west coast cleanliness and precision. Yet, while Tyler maintained to a journalist that 'a modern look comes of using modern materials and working in modern cities with modern ideas',[14] he presented his headquarters in an 1850 coach house thirty-five miles north of New York City in quite a different way. In an interview with Susan DeChillo of the *New York Times*, he pointed out how much Tyler Graphics differed from Gemini:

> It's a country shop, a quiet place. There are fewer people. What happens here happens slowly. The shop is not on a time schedule as it was in California. Here the editions are much smaller . . . we're not interested in numbers.[15]

However much this description may suggest U.L.A.E. in Tanya Grosman's heyday, the Bedford Village operation is actually very different. At the beginning of 1985, Tyler had fourteen employees including six printers between the ages of twenty-seven and forty — Rodney Konopaki, Lee Funderburg, Roger Campbell, Tom Strianese, Steve Reeves and Bob Cross. Most of the printers had been with him for over five years and Tyler was proud of the record:

> We're talking about cottage industries . . . with all the problems of business, with responsibilities where you take care of people. You don't just suddenly hire and fire, or run an itinerant situation. Things have stabilized a little bit. We've got seven- and eight-year-old veterans. That's pretty good, to have people in one spot for that period of time.[16]

The possibility of embracing the complete range of media, even in a single print, became one of the hallmarks of Tyler's new workshop. Kathan Brown, who has restricted her own operation at Crown Point Press (in Oakland, California) to etching, is in general critical of the tendency that developed in American workshops during the 1970s, because she feels several shops offered techniques they had not fully mastered. She concedes, however, that Tyler is one of the few printers who could operate successfully in this way, because of his 'amazingly technically-oriented mind'.[17] In fact, the Bedford Village workshop is equipped with a dazzling array of machinery; Tyler has one of the most sophisticated presses available — a DUFA VII Steinmesse and Stollberg flatbed offset press. Made by a German manufacturer, it has refinements that Tyler specially requested, including a refrigerated bed that keeps the work on metal lithographic plates cool and therefore open. It is versatile enough to accommodate stone, type-high blocks or wood in any thickness from a wafer to 3½ inches. The most radical development at Bedford Village, however, was not in the area of up-to-the-minute technology, but in Tyler's involvement with the centuries-old craft of hand papermaking.

plates 64-65

THE EXPLORATION OF PAPER

Judith Goldman has shrewdly observed that Tyler's interest in paper is the parable of his career. In 1963 he was trying to find the standard sheet for editions. Ten years later, he was encouraging artists to convert the very substance of paper into unique works of art.

Although by the mid-sixties Tamarind was recommending ten different papers for use in lithography, it had approved only four — Arches Cover paper in two colours, Rives BFK, German copperplate and Inomachi Nacre — in its first year. In 1962, by which time its research programme was well under way, the Workshop had established a nomenclature for describing the properties of paper and had begun the task of trying to ensure a stable and reliable supply for edition printing. During Tyler's sojourn at Tamarind from 1963 to 1965, he conducted many tests into the capacity of different papers. He investigated their absorption, their ability to accept pressure in multiple or embossed printings and, by virtue of their light-fastness and low acidity, the likelihood that they could survive as art. During the 1960s, when editions tended to be quite large and a brilliant whiteness was often important for both colour field and Pop aesthetics, the neutral and dependable papers Tamarind had first identified were suitable for most purposes. Although all were imported, they formed the substrate for the majority of American prints.

Certainly this was the case at Gemini, although from her earliest days at U.L.A.E. Tanya Grosman had used a far greater variety of papers. When Jasper Johns first went to Gemini, his lithographs had already been issued by U.L.A.E. on about twenty different surfaces. It was Johns who showed Tyler some handmade papers that had been sent by Fred Siegenthaler of Basel, but both Johns and Rauschenberg knew that, at least for the largest scale on which they were working, mould-made papers would have to be used.

In his address to the World Print Council paper conference in San Francisco, Tyler explained that in the early days of his west coast company he had little experience of printing on handmade papers. Most artists of the day were content to work with mould-made papers and 'in many cases the handmade paper of this time was so beautiful and so powerful in its surface that it intimidated not only me, but the artists'.[1] Tyler used handmade papers almost exclusively for trial proofs and apart from introducing an occasional variant, such as Japanese paper or the English graph paper used for Stella's *Stars of Persia*, the staple ingredient of Gemini editioning was imported Rives or Arches. Indeed, Tyler estimated that of the 700 editions, totalling 54,000 impressions, that he had been responsible for producing between 1965 and 1978, only 170 editions, totalling some 13,000 impressions, were on handmade paper.[2]

Because he believed so profoundly that scale had to be increased if prints were to be taken seriously (despite some evidence from Rembrandt to the contrary), Tyler entered with characteristic energy into his own paper research from the moment he had his own shop. His aim was to encourage various manufacturers of European papers imported into America to supply good mould-made papers in rolls, so that the larger sizes needed at Gemini could be cut. Such is the tradition of deckle-edged sheet manufacture in handmade papers that Arjomari, a company which eventually supplied what Tyler wanted, was manufacturing mould-made papers in a continuous strip and then tearing them to pretend that they had been created as separate sheets! Another amusing story about Tyler's 'paper-chase' was related by Bernard Guerlain, president of a company that imported French papers into America. During a visit to the Arches mill in France, Tyler insisted on a paper as brilliantly white as one of the

plate 4

samples he was shown, but was told that he could not have it, as such a paper was only available in February, when the frozen ground of the Vosges mountains releases no silt into the water. Because of the need for a standardized product, the company usually tinted its February batch to reconcile it with the rest. However, because Tyler ordered the entire making, the company did in the end produce a special 'February paper' for Gemini.[3]

Shopping abroad was expensive, however, and in 1967 Tyler began the search for an American manufacturer who could produce an adequate paper for fine art. With Larry Hardy of the Zellerbach·Paper Corporation as consultant, Tyler entered into extensive research with the makers of an archival book paper, hoping to make a fine art paper with a 'friendly feel'. In February 1969, he ran five hours of tests, using three pulp formulas, with yet another paper manufacturer. Despite these efforts, which Hardy described as 'heroic', the National Endowment for the Arts, part of whose grant had funded the research, had to be told that the hope of a domestic supply of a suitable paper was very slim, as 'the art market does not possess the shimmering goal of dollar value'.[4] The scale of American papermaking was so huge that the consumption of a fine art paper would simply not have been large enough to justify its manufacture.

Arjomari, however, provided the rolls of paper used for Rauschenberg's *Stoned moon* and in 1969 they sent Tyler a ticket to France. When he eventually made the journey to Europe, Tyler, guided by Elie d'Humières and Vera Freeman, was able to clinch regular supplies of Arjomari mould-made papers and at the same time became aware of other possibilities. Another stimulus came from Japan early in 1970 when the printer was installing Oldenburg's *Icebag* there. During his trip, he visited Kyoto and saw examples of dye-coloured papers by Japanese craftsmen. The third piece of the papermaking jigsaw fell into place when, in April 1970, Tyler was artist in residence at Cranbrook Academy, Michigan. Laurence Barker, who had learned the craft from Douglass Howell, papermaker for such projects as U.L.A.E.'s *Stones*, was then head of Cranbrook's printmaking department and had set up the first University paper mill in 1963. Tyler gave Barker an order to make some paper for Gemini, but, as he was packing to leave America for Spain, Barker passed on the job to his graduate assistant, John Koller, who supplied sheets that were used for two of Lichtenstein's 1930s heads. The introduction to Koller later proved important, for by the time Tyler left Gemini for the east coast, Koller and his wife Kathy had set up H.M.P. Papers in Woodstock Valley, Connecticut, not very far from the printer's new facility.

It is difficult to pinpoint the precise moment when artists stopped seeing paper merely as the background or carrier of an image and began to realize that it could become art by itself. In the 1940s, Douglass Howell had made drawings by embedding thread in pulp at the wet stage. By 1962 in Europe, Isabel Echarri was moulding sculptured reliefs by couching[5] sheets of handmade pulp onto a shaped form. The growing interest in an art form in which technique and medium were inseparable, which began to ignite in America in the late 1960s, was certainly related to the progressive analysis of artistic means. Tyler knew of Howell and other papermakers like Joe Wilfer, but because he saw paper simply as a substrate, he dismissed what both of them were doing as rather 'artsy craftsy'. By 1972, in the feminist climate which even led to the acceptance of 'woman's work' such as sewing, dyeing and weaving as legitimate ways of making fine art, Wilfer was collaborating with the printmaker Bill Weegee and the artist Alan Shields.[6] Within a few years, Tyler himself was responding enthusiastically at his new Bedford Village facility to Shields' offbeat and idiosyncratic strategies and was making hand-sewn, hand-knotted, perforated weavings and lattices of handmade paper, stamped with every conceivable kind of printing block and plate (and some inconceivable ones, too, ranging from laser-cut woodblocks to bathtub drain plugs and pencil erasers). Even Shields' relatively traditional tusche lithographs were drawn with eye droppers and matchsticks.

Tyler undertook his first major handmade paper project, however, before he left Gemini. The trip to Bordeaux and Epinal in France gave him the idea of hiring a mill for a few days and taking an artist to work there with him. He resolved to choose a major artist and a large project and then arrange a loud fanfare to publicize it. When he ran through a list of possibilities, he decided that the artist who 'could invent on the spot, had a lot of ideas and loved the challenge', was Robert Rauschenberg, who, as he expected, was 'tickled to death'[7] by the idea. Consequently, in the summer of 1973, Rauschenberg spent four days in the Richard de Bas mill in Ambert, south-east of Aubusson in the Auvergne.

In February 1983, Rauschenberg told an audience at the Japanese International Paper Conference in Kyoto that he had found pulp 'particularly seductive'. The Ambert mill, however, 'had been built in 1200 and hadn't changed a bit' and wearing wooden shoes on an irregular stone floor in wet conditions had been 'like spending twelve hours a day in frozen yoghurt'.[8]

plate 62

Rauschenberg believes in a minimum of planning for any project and in allowing art to grow out of a response to conditions, materials and process. Throughout his stay in France, people were telling him: 'That's not the way you do it', but 'the works turned out all right!'. The artist told Joseph Young that he liked working 'blind' and was not involved in expression, but rather was striving for 'productive anonymity'. The only predetermined ideas he had when he went to France were a desire to make the form the print and to paint with paper.[9]

For five *Pages*, Rauschenberg mixed up five natural shades of bleached and un-bleached rag pulp, which is a slurry of beaten fibres suspended in water. *Page one*, for example, was a free form resembling a tree or an atomic cloud, in which Rauschenberg embedded pieces of the rag similar to those used as an ingredient in the pulp.

For other works, Rauschenberg asked the local plumber and tinsmith to make shapes like outsize cookie cutters from his designs. These were placed as containing devices on the traditional wove paper moulds, wire bottomed trays in which the 'stuff' is scooped from the vat, allowing the water to escape through the mesh so that the damp residue of wet pulped fibre forms a sheet. These sheets are flipped out in a deft movement known as couching, which transfers them onto interleaving layers of felt. At Ambert, the felts gently supported Rauschenberg's sheets and helped to extract excess moisture as they were squeezed in the mill's early fourteenth century press.

In addition to the five unadorned *Pages*, Rauschenberg made a set of colourful works known as *Fuses* in which brilliant water-soluble Swiss dyes were used to colour the pulp, causing one area of the sheet to bleed into another when they were pressed. Rauschenberg had asked Gemini to screenprint some Japanese tissue with media images and these were patted onto appropriate areas of the *Fuses*, bonding them to the 'bubble bath' of wet pulp.

The innovatory nature of the project brought the whole matter of editioning into question, for in some cases Rauschenberg created a set of unique but related pieces, while in others he made prototypes which assistants then went on to repeat. Tyler and his wife, Kay, were both heavily involved in the project, together with Robert Petersen and two French paper makers. Before he left Ambert, Rauschenberg had created about one-third of the three hundred paperworks that were eventually distributed.

When *Newsweek* published its special issue on the state of the arts in America, showing Rauschenberg working at the Ambert mill, Joe Wilfer was understandably chagrined to think that while he had been making paper for years with Weegee and Shields in Wisconsin, an article that purported to be about the state of the arts in the United States featured an artist working at a French mill![10] Nevertheless, the publicity had its effect. By the end of the 1970s, as Rauschenberg pointed out in Japan, few artists had not been touched by 'the paper revolution' and the study of paper became a required course in a number of American art schools. For Rauschenberg, the Ambert experience was merely an introduction to the field. Several other international paper projects — including one in India and another in China — followed. By the time *Pages* and *Fuses* were actually published, however, Tyler had left the west coast and was planning to steep himself up to the elbows in other vats.

PAPER IN BEDFORD VILLAGE

plate 2
Asked how Gemini's philosophy had changed since Tyler left the shop, one of his former partners, Sidney Felsen, said that instead of collaboration being handled by one man, it was now spread among all of Gemini's printers, and that the workshop supported artists by 'researching and responding to what they want rather than developing a technology and then "selling" it to them'.[1] The first part of Felsen's observation has a very attractive democratic ring to it and acknowledges the fact that, however much public relations focuses on a figurehead, the actual work is always done by many unacknowledged hands. The second part of Felsen's statement accords, however, with the perhaps less democratic convention that the artist alone calls all the shots and that the correct procedure for the lesser mortal — the artisan or craftsman — is to respond and not to lead. What is left unsaid in all of this is the difficulty of inventing a process and selling it if there is no longer a 'technological wizard' in-house.

While it is certainly true that very little of value is likely to emerge from printmaking without the image-creating ability and wholehearted involvement of artists, it is worth asking whether Rauschenberg would, on his own initiative, have pushed the production of paper to arrive at the scale that graphic art eventually encompassed. Would these developments have occurred if the artist had made lithographs only at U.L.A.E.? And while the brilliance of Rauschenberg's performance in France was emulated by other artists world-wide, would the Ambert project, and by extension the other projects that followed, ever have taken place without the enthusiasm and vision of a particular printer?

Some of Tyler's prints would probably have appeared in similar form whoever had editioned them, and there are many collaborative postures for artists to adopt between leading and being pushed. Conversely, there are also a number of projects — perhaps a greater number in the case of Tyler than of any other printer — where the ambition and complexity of the final product makes it clear that it has taken two to tango and leaves a question in the mind as to the identity of the choreographer.

The first years in Bedford Village were a struggle, for Tyler had to equip himself from scratch. At Albers' own request, the first project he undertook in the east was in screenprinting. Then as specially modified or custom-built presses were delivered, the nature of the work Tyler undertook was able to expand. In his second year on the east coast, the printer, with the assistance of John Koller at H.M.P., embarked on his second paper project and made 183 paper pulp reliefs with Frank Stella.

Stella's titles are often elegiac and, among other things, commemorate nineteenth-century clipper ships, defunct mines, ancient cities, extinct birds and dead racing drivers. The paper reliefs he made at Bedford Village were based on the Polish village
plate 63
series — paintings with tilted planes named after eighteenth-century wooden synagogues that had been destroyed in Poland and Russia during the second world war. Betty Fiske and Tyler's daughter, Kim, sewed three-dimensional mesh moulds with brass wire, based on Stella's maquettes. Then, using the first proofs from each mould as trials, the artist worked the pulp while it was wet, dyeing it, collaging other papers onto it and later, when it was dry, painting it with casein, watercolour and more dye. The Kollers completed the pieces.

The following year, Ellsworth Kelly also worked with Koller and Tyler in paper, applying a layer of coloured pulp through elegantly shaped moulds of arcs and curves, placed over wet base sheets. The moulds were removed before the sheets were pressed, at which stage the intense palette of coloured dyes, which Tyler had devel-

61 Betty Fiske working on a Ron Davis project in 1975

62 Tyler and Rauschenberg at the Richard de Bas paper mill in Ambert, France, during the 1973 *Pages and fuses* project

63 Frank Stella: *Kozangródek II* from the *Paper relief* series, 1975, 26 x 21½ x 1¾ in (66.0 x 54.6 x 4.4 cm), one of 183 uniquely coloured paperworks in six editioned configurations

64 Lindsay Green and Ken Tyler forming a sheet of paper for the Kenneth Noland project, 1978

65 Lindsay Green and Ken Tyler couching a newly formed sheet of paper for the *Horizontal stripe* series by Kenneth Noland in 1978

oped for the project, bled from one area of the paper to another, rather like Rauschenberg's *Fuses*. Kelly's achievement was hailed in *Artforum* in 1977 as 'a new sensuousness and a release from the drawn line'. Altogether, the artist made prototypes for editions of a dozen rectangular sheets and eight smaller, squarish images in colours ranging from vivid primaries to the most subtle neutrals.

Just as he had increased the scale of graphics in the 1960s, so now Tyler became involved in the increased scale involved in painting with paper. Kenneth Noland, one side of whose largest paperworks eventually measured more than four feet, wanted to make sheets larger than Koller could accommodate, and Tyler realized that he could not ensure Koller sufficient business to warrant enlarging his facility. Nevertheless, he had 'a keen desire to offer this particular artist the scale he wanted',[2] and he decided to tool up himself. His garage in Los Angeles had been pressed into service for Oldenburg's *Airflow* — now in Bedford Village it became the paper studio, equipped with a Hollander-type beater, a press, a couching table, and an array of plastic pails, rubber aprons and wellington boots. Never one to do things by halves, Tyler (and Lindsay Green, who was to become his second wife) researched not only occidental methods but oriental ones as well. Kozo, Gampi, and Mitsumata fibres were imported and, adding to its western antique laid and wove moulds with deckles, the workshop also equipped itself with flexible bamboo screens from the east.

plate 64

plate 68

Kenneth Noland began work with Tyler in April 1978 and eventually created two hundred unique images. He had made a screenprint in 1969, but had never taken to printmaking; like his friend the sculptor, David Smith, he disliked the concept of reproducibility. In 1976, however, he had been master in residence at a papermaking workshop in Garner Tullis' institute set up in 1973 in San Francisco and had become sufficiently enamoured of the process to install his own papermaking studio.

What now attracted the artist to continue in the medium was the fact that each paper image could be subtly differentiated. Moreover, papermaking gave him 'new access to touch',[3] and allowed him to manipulate and dye the stuff of paper in a way that related directly to his method of staining raw cotton duck with paint, where the colour is put *into* the ground. Although he used basic moulds for his series of circular targets, horizontally striped and diagonally striped images, each was a unique variant, utilizing different colours in anything from three to eight layers. Occasionally monotype screen or lithographic printings were added after the paper had dried. The colours of the pulp ranged from bold and particularly intense shades, like the superb Madonna blue, to subtle pinks, peaches, salmons and duck-egg greens. Sometimes small shreds of paper, wool or silk were sprinkled into the pulp to emphasize the surface, and transparent films were set down so that the earlier layers receded as if behind a window pane frosted with breath.[4]

plates 65-66

plate 67

Soon after Noland's project was completed, David Hockney happened to be passing through New York. Having just designed *The Magic Flute*, and therefore familiar with the inevitable compromises that a group activity entails, he was in fact in flight from collaborative enterprise and en route for a period of solitary painting in California, 'where they leave you alone'.[5] Before leaving England, however, he had lost his driving licence and, while waiting for a new one to reach him in New York, he went to tell Ken Tyler (who was pressing him to make some lithographs) that on no account was he going to make prints. It was then that Tyler showed him the new Noland and Kelly paperworks and Hockney had to agree that they were 'stunningly beautiful'. The artist was seduced into staying 'three days' to 'try it out'. Forty-five days and a great many paperworks later, Hockney finally resumed his journey.

The artist's first task in coming to grips with the new medium was to abandon any idea of finicky drawing and to think in bold colour areas — a tough adjustment for an essentially linear draughtsman. Then he realized that working in pulp was totally unlike graphic process 'in that I had to make each and every work myself' (although it's only fair to add that Ken Tyler and Lindsay Green did provide a little help here and there!).

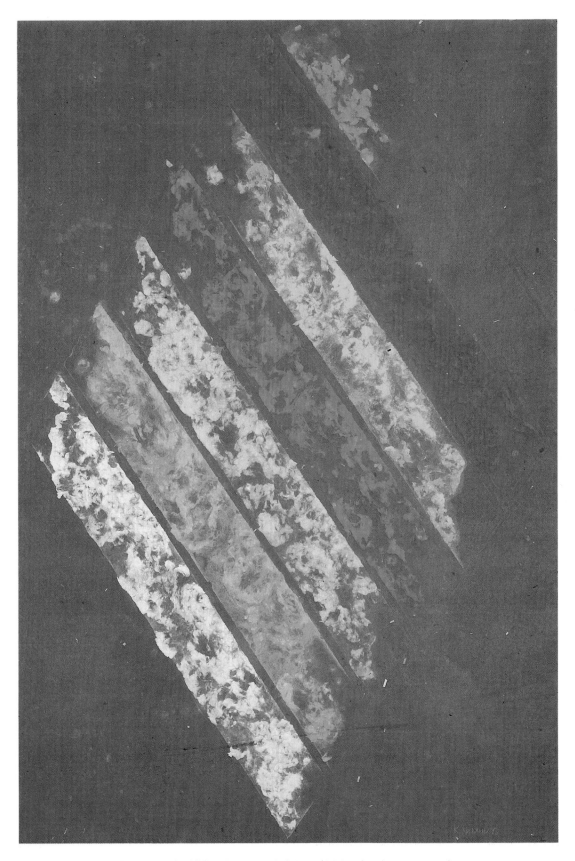

66   Kenneth Noland: *Diagonal stripe VI-9*, 1978, 50 x 32 in (124.0 x 84.4 cm), unique paperwork

67 John Hutcheson printing a unique lithographic addition to one of Kenneth Noland's paperworks in the *Circle series*, 1978

68 A flexible oriental bamboo screen being used for one of Kenneth Noland's *Circle series* paperworks

69 David Hockney and Ken Tyler

In attempting to escape his tendency to fussiness and to make use of the essential characteristics of the medium, Hockney suggested that, since the size Noland had used was about the maximum size that Tyler could make,[6] he could arrange six or even more sheets and treat them as one dramatic composition. Obligingly, Tyler built a platform in his driveway large enough to accommodate the basic multisheet iconography following the artist's simple reed pen drawings. The pictorial shapes were defined by galvanized iron containing walls, rather like cloisonné enamel on a grand scale. Hockney overcame the reservations he had previously had about working in series, and used each basic form for a number of variations.

Prompted by the sight of Ursula, the shop cat, falling into a vat, he had decided that a watery medium needed a watery subject.[7] Tyler's pool, beside which artist and printer used to take lunch, suggested itself as the obvious subject. The near impossibility of depicting water had always fascinated Hockney. Now, in the same way that Monet's waterlily paintings featured the water's surface, as well as reflections from above it and forms perceived underneath, he used the pool and its diving-board as a vehicle for reflecting different weather conditions and different times of day. As Hockney's visit extended into autumn, the lido blues and greens ruffled, mottled and were eventually clouded by rain, growing murkier as the days shortened. In four mysterious night versions, the scene became an enchanted harmony of cobalt and petrol blue, with a black instead of a yellow diving-board. In one of the most adventurous compositions of all, its dozen sheets spanning over fourteen feet in width, Hockney's friend Gregory is seen diving into the pool. The artist depicted his water-

plate 70

plate 73

plates 71, 74

70 Tyler and David Hockney (with Ursula the shop cat) during the *Paper pools* project in 1978

distorted form, frozen by the camera and looking 'like a lobster or a crab', by kneading handfuls of pink 'stuff' as one might squeeze flesh itself.

In the end, Hockney forgot about escaping to California to paint, because he realized that was exactly what he was already doing. He knew that if he were painting in the normal way he 'wouldn't have the nerve just to throw it around like this and pour it on'. Nor if he had had to stretch canvases himself would he have been as swift to tear up those that misfired. As well as spooning on the colour, he applied it by turkey baster and brush. Most importantly, the paperworks encouraged him to be more audacious and to go straight to the essence of the picture, avoiding the distraction of detail; eventually, the experience helped him considerably with his other work.

Hockney's engaging account of his experiences, illustrated with many drawings of

plates 1, 72   Tyler and Lindsay Green as they fetch and carry for him, is very revealing. One becomes aware of Tyler's cleverness in seducing Hockney in the first place, of his endless patience in teaching him all the possibilities of paperwork and then responding to the painter's own inventiveness, of his willingness to resort to a little con trick (which didn't fool Hockney for a moment) when he ran out of a certain blue, of his ingenuity in overcoming any technical difficulty, but above all of his inexhaustible energy for a great deal of very tiring work. Hockney wrote:

> I have never worked with anybody with more energy. It was fantastic. He was willing to work any hours. It didn't matter . . . Working with someone who has an awful lot of energy is very thrilling. With Kenneth Tyler, nothing was impossible. If I said, could we, he said, yes, yes, it can be done.[8]

71

72

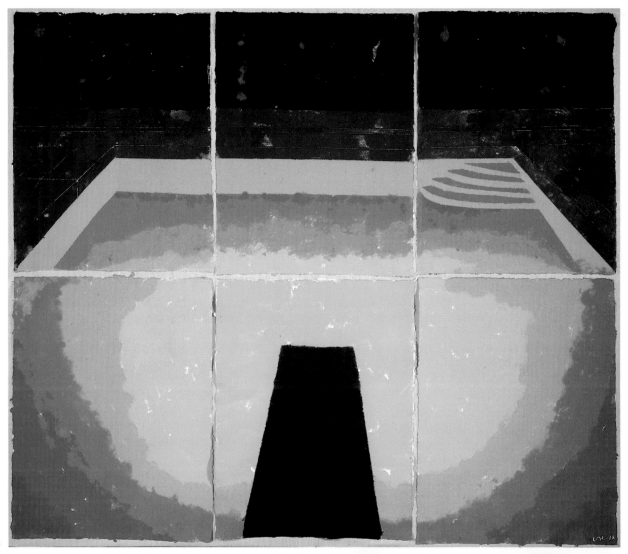

71 David Hockney: *A diver, Paper pool 17*, 1978, 12 abutted sheets (6 shown) overall 72 x 171 in (182.8 x 434.3 cm), unique paperwork

72 Hockney drawing with dye from a kitchen baster on newly formed sheets of paper pulp prepared by Ken Tyler and Lindsay Green for the *Paper pools* project

73 David Hockney: *Midnight pool, Paper pool 30*, 1978, 71 x 82½ in (180.3 x 209.5 cm), unique paperwork

74 Ken Tyler and Lindsay Green positioning newly formed sheets for one of Hockney's 12 panel *Paper pools*

THE PAINTER-PRINTMAKERS

Intuitive abstract painters, who carefully define themselves as 'artists' rather than 'printmakers', must be among the most difficult people to print for. Tyler's proven ability to work successfully with Robert Motherwell and Helen Frankenthaler (who made her first *absolutely* convincing graphic statement in Bedford Village) is therefore a measure of the sensibility and tact that he, as a naturally impetuous and even impatient man, has been able to school in himself over the years.

The realization that any graphic mark is made at one remove and can never be closer than first cousin to the spontaneity that gave it birth, together with the fact that they conceived of the artist's studio as an intensely private place, has always deterred Abstract Expressionists from making prints. Although Motherwell has welcomed the camaraderie of a print shop as a break from solitude, he is, unlike Robert Rauschenberg's generation, far from seeing it as an occasion for a performance or a happening. Indeed, in 1979, he described his terror upon arriving at a printer/publisher to find a huge body of people waiting, and realizing 'with a sinking heart that an enormous amount of time and money and organization has been set aside in a definite time-slot for you to be a creative genius. Now there's no situation that freezes your blood more . . .'[1]

One suspects that this description fits Motherwell's first visit to Gemini in 1973, for Tyler once said that where Motherwell was concerned he had had to throw away all preconceived ideas about production, as such a strategy had worked 'only the first time, because he was on *my* turf in California. It's never worked since'.[2]

Motherwell, for his part, has made it clear that the lithographic collages he made in Los Angeles were fraught with difficulties; doubtless the predetermined nature of a printed collage had something to do with his reservations. Sam Wagstaff who, when he was curator of the Wadsworth Atheneum published the first version of a Motherwell collage in a screenprinted portfolio of 1964, used the ladies of the museum's voluntary committee to tear identical shapes of paper for the 550 copies of the edition. Motherwell looked speechlessly at the finished print for fifteen minutes and then said: 'It scares me!'.[3] It was perhaps with similar emotion that the artist decided the prints of the *Summer light series* he had made in California were 'too suave' and 'a parody of himself'.[4] Despite the commercial success of the collage prints, he felt the six *Soot black stone* lithographs, on a French Hawthorne of Larroque paper that Tyler had had specially watermarked for him with his initials, were the *real* Motherwell.

Nevertheless, Motherwell was among the first artists to work with Tyler after he moved east. The painter's studio in Greenwich, Connecticut, is only a few miles from Bedford Village and in 1974 he and Tyler collaborated on an exquisite lithograph that Motherwell called *The stoneness of the stone*. Tyler remembers that day because it was 'magical from the start' and 'everything worked'.[5] The two gestural marks that the artist made with brushloads of tusche looked so exactly right that Tyler, not yet set up to make paper himself, conceived the happy idea of ordering a sheet that would recapture exactly the shape of the surface on which Motherwell had originally worked. This was made in two tones of grey, laminated together at the wet stage, by Twinrocker of Indiana.

plates 81, 75

Later the same year, Tyler tried to overcome some of Motherwell's problems with printed collage by photographically enlarging the cigarette wrappers the artist liked to use and uniting them with automatist gestures on a large scale. *Bastos*, a volatile print so big it needed several printers to handle it, was one of the results. Between 1976 and 1978, however, despite the grandeur of his Bedford Village prints, Motherwell,

plate 85
plates 76-78, 80

75 Motherwell and Tyler testing the consistency of lithographic tusche before making *The stoneness of the stone*

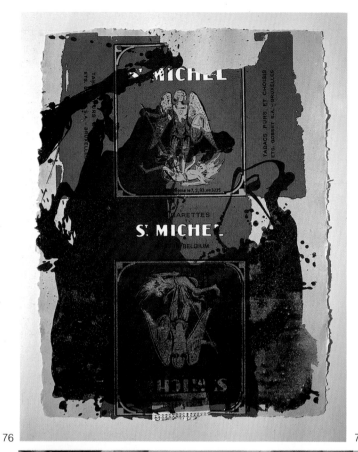

76

77

78

76 Robert Motherwell: *Bastos*, 1974/5, 62¼ x 40 in (158.1 x 101.6 cm), lithograph, edition 49

77 Robert Motherwell: *St Michael III*, 1975-79, 41½ x 31½ in (105.4 x 80.0 cm), lithograph, screenprint, edition 99

78 Ken Tyler screenprinting Motherwell's *St Michael III*, 1979

79 Robert Motherwell: *America-La France, Variation VII*, 1984, 52¾ x 36 in (134 x 91.4 cm), lithograph, collage, edition 68

80 Robert Motherwell: *Tobacco Roth-Händle*, 1974/75, 41 x 31 in (104.1 x 78.7 cm), lithograph, screenprint, edition 45

81 Robert Motherwell: *The stoneness of the stone*, 1974, 41 x 30 in (104.1 x 76.2 cm), lithograph on two-tone paper, edition 75

82 Ken Tyler collaging an element for Motherwell's *America-La France, Variation IV*, 1984

in retreat from the pressure of publishers and wanting to make graphic art 'on impulse rather than by appointment', set up a personal lithographic printer in his own studio to join the intaglio printer already there. He resumed collaboration at Bedford Village in 1979, although he now began the more comfortable arrangement of working in Tyler's shop on weekend afternoons. He would then take proofs home with him so that he could think about them in the peace of his own studio and gauge their quality in the context of his other work.

The lesson Tyler had to learn from Motherwell was the hardest possible for a man of his inventive impetuosity — it was, quite simply, that he should leave the artist alone. After Motherwell had drawn a number of stones, wielding his brush like 'a Japanese killer',[6] Tyler would hover around waiting to be given something on which to work:

> You've got your hyperkinetic body running overtime and you're trying to look very calm and relaxed. And once in a while he'll look over and say: 'I know you want this stone. Go do something. Leave me alone'.[7]

83   Robert Motherwell: *Gipsy curse*, 1983, one of 19 illuminations from the book *El negro* 15 x 15 in (38.2 x 38.2 cm), lithograph on red and white paper, edition 98

84 Robert Motherwell, *Forever black*, 1981-83, one of 19 illuminations from the book *El negro*, 15 x 37¾ in (38.2 x 95.8 cm), lithograph, edition 51

The waiting periods during which the artist came to terms with his own work were particularly hard for Tyler because of his desire to make a contribution. He found it difficult to accept that 'being there and not doing a damned thing' was helping. Eventually he discovered that 'You just have to be able to shut up and print whatever you're given, and not try to make it into something else. And that's usually difficult for a printer'.[8]

When the catalogue raisonné of his prints was first published, Motherwell, in a gesture of unbounded respect towards his many collaborators, allowed them to have their say about his graphic work. The book was in effect a tribute to those printers who frequently became his alter ego. He acknowledged that with their help '. . . in many cases the work became better . . . the master craftsman with all his detailed refinements, plus the startling magic of a thing beautifully executed, can improve the artist's original vision'.[9] He had already told an interviewer that '. . . in making prints, one's full depth of appreciation for the marvelousness of craftsmanship is enormously reinforced. And I like first-rate craftsmen as human beings as well as any group of people I know'.[10]

plates 83-84

Between 1980 and 1983, Motherwell worked at Tyler Graphics on his second artist's book, drawing nineteen lithographs to illuminate *El negro Motherwell*. This poem, written in the artist's honour by the Spanish poet, Rafael Alberti, dealt with Motherwell's inexhaustible fascination for 'the mystery of black'. 'What more natural', Motherwell asked in 1979, 'than a passionate interest in juxtaposing black and white, being and non-being, life and death?'.[11] Motherwell had already made a book of another of Alberti's poems, *A la pintura*, which was published by U.L.A.E. and hailed as a masterwork in an exhibition at the Metropolitan Museum of Art. Despite its magisterial conception, the book's sheets are somewhat stiff and awkward and the platemark of the etching distorts the paper, giving it a sense of strain. The beautiful off-white sheets for *El negro*, fashioned in Tyler's own mill, are a great deal more sympathetic and satisfying to handle.

plate 79

In 1983/84, Motherwell celebrated his European affiliations by making a series of nine lithographic collages called *America — la France*. These collages are based on labels from Arjomari Prioux, exquisitely arranged amidst shafts of colour from various other handmade papers, lucidly articulated by crayon and framed by lithographic washes in the subtlest neutrals. Newly completed, these were on view at the Walker Art Center in Minneapolis in September 1984 when Motherwell helped open and dedicate the Center's study facility devoted to Tyler's work. In a moving tribute,

Motherwell revealed that the Sunday afternoons he regularly spent with the printer had been among the happiest of his life. He said:

85   Ken Tyler and Robert Motherwell discussing the proofing of *Lament for Lorca* in 1982

> Although I am married to painting, printing is my mistress . . . my time off. My involvement would have been relatively modest if Tyler hadn't happened to move two or three miles away with fantastic presses and printers. He is the greatest technical genius in America, probably in the world for all I know . . . an artistic Don Juan, fascinating and seducing you . . . companionable, understanding, helpful and eager to see this miracle of making something appear in front of your eyes.[12]

While Motherwell says he looked to collaborative printmaking as a method of self-transcendence able to contribute a further dimension to 'one's habitual conditioned ways of doing things', Helen Frankenthaler has been at pains to impose her will as a painter on her lithographs and etchings. Judith Goldman has described Frankenthaler's prints as 'obstinately non-graphic', for the essence of her painting is the spontaneously generated mark which she hopes will look 'as if it happened all at once'. This characteristic places her images in direct opposition to the requirements of sophisticated printmaking.

When Tanya Grosman invited Helen Frankenthaler to U.L.A.E. in 1961 to make her first lithographs, the artist was suspicious of printmaking, regarding it as old-fashioned. She can still be ambivalent on the subject, stressing 'that she is essentially a painter and that she is not interested in the techniques of printmaking: 'I am not interested in the patience it requires. I am not interested in the chemistry. I want it done for me, but I have to be there for every hairline of the doing'.[13]

Although all painters trying to distinguish themselves from illustrators stress their indifference to technique, Thomas Krens, who edited the catalogue raisonné of Frankenthaler's prints, feels that Tanya Grosman's encouragement of that attitude had ironically reinforced the artist's aversion to the mechanics of printmaking on the mistaken grounds that it encumbered the creative act. Krens felt that Frankenthaler's indifference to specifics of technique prevented her from involving herself in the various processes sufficiently to understand the possibilities of printmaking. Krens observed that:

> All great printmakers through history have been intimately involved in the process of the medium and able to work through the inherent potential by the techniques they used. As a result of the strength of her conviction about painting, Frankenthaler was never able to involve herself fully in the process, to overcome the inherent resistance of the techniques to her ideas and consistently make great prints — at least, until the woodcuts of the seventies.[14]

Tyler had invited Frankenthaler to make prints when he was at Gemini and she even visited the workshop in California, but as she was already devoted to Tanya Grosman, and did not want 'to conquer the world with her prints',[15] she refused the invitation. Tyler realized that Gemini — which must have looked to Frankenthaler like a business-oriented art factory — was wrong for her personality:

> Helen knew I admired her and wanted to make prints with her, but it didn't work out. Perhaps the shop was too slick. We did a certain thing at a certain time. It just didn't fit Helen's temperament.[16]

plate 86

When Tyler set up Tyler Graphics in Bedford Village, Frankenthaler came at last to work with him and he has given an account of the artist's unusual and laborious working method. 'The most complicated form of printmaking', it consists of filling seven or eight stones with marks and then, irrespective of the enormous difficulties involved in registering them, cutting up and collaging proofs together until she hits upon a suitable arrangement. Tyler said: 'We proof various stones in partial combinations, we wrap them, we change them, we turn them upside-down, they're moved all over the place . . .'[17] Frankenthaler expects the printer to be willing to try out a shape in fifty different places, on twenty different papers and with as many different mauves as may be necessary to get the image exactly right. Unless the workshop does this and eventually satisfies her, the print is scratched and she will not sign it.

86 Helen Frankenthaler in 1977

87 Helen Frankenthaler: *Essence mulberry*, 1977, 40 x 18½ in (101.6 x 46.9 cm), woodcut, edition 46

Tyler has learned that for Frankenthaler, as for Motherwell, he must not 'invade the image-making act', but must simply serve it. He admires Frankenthaler's perseverance and believes 'she should get a lot of credit' for battling on until her prints work. She has reinforced the lesson he has had to learn that for some artists collaboration involves knowing who can benefit from being pushed technically, and who cannot:

> As you guide artists through the maze, you determine who has a mind for it and who doesn't. If I decide an artist, for whatever reason, cannot cope with a technique, then I alter my presentation and keep all mechanical functions to a minimum.[18]

plate 87

When Frankenthaler first worked with Tyler in lithography and in etching, her methods were similar to those she had used elsewhere. It was only when she tried the much less tractable woodcut, that the character of her work necessarily changed. At U.L.A.E., she had made a few beautiful woodcuts which simply juxtaposed areas of colour in a jig-saw fashion. When she came to make *Essence mulberry* at Tyler's workshop, however, she at last departed from an excessive reliance on the kind of mark-making characteristic of painting and began to realize her full graphic potential. The subtle blends of colour she worked with may have been suggested by a Hiroshige woodcut from her own New York apartment, while she was certainly also influenced by an exhibition of early German woodcuts at the Metropolitan Museum. She was also inspired by the colour of the juice from a mulberry tree in Tyler's garden. Whatever the sources of the image, 'The whole print, the notion, the title, the method and the feel of it was from the heart and core'.[19]

'NO schmaltz pliz!', the artist wrote on an early state,[20] while she inscribed the right-to-print proof in the Australian National Gallery collection with the words: 'Go! I like it!'. In this work, Tyler declared, Frankenthaler had at last decided that a print could be as good as a painting.

RECENT DEVELOPMENTS AT
BEDFORD VILLAGE

Many artists — Michael Heizer, Richard Smith,[1] Ed Baynard, Nancy Graves, Richard Hamilton and Stanley Boxer — have made beautiful but relatively traditional prints at Bedford Village, but their prints have shown no particular desire to expand graphic technology. More surprisingly, some who were previously Gemini's most tech-nologically-oriented artists — among them Claes Oldenburg and Roy Lichtenstein — have been equally traditional in their work. Oldenburg's output has so far been limited to a nine-colour lithograph called *Chicago stuffed with numbers*, while Roy Lichtenstein, after completing his 'industrial' *Entablatures*, based on classical architec-tural forms in America, turned to handmade woodcuts and etchings relating to his paintings on Red Indian themes. Lichtenstein said that he had originally wanted his prints to be 'very simple and mechanical' without traditionally elegant refinements; he now wanted them to be less concerned with precision and he felt that woodcut was the ideal material to prevent him from making things 'perfect'.[2]

plates 88-92

plates 93-97

Those artists who have had the most extensive and long-standing involvement with Tyler have tended to push printmaking furthest towards its potential as a fully creative medium independent of painting.

In September 1984, immediately after the opening of the facility devoted to his archive in Minneapolis, Tyler went to Mexico with David Hockney to begin a new project. During one of his many journeys, the artist's car had broken down in Acatlan, 150 miles south of Mexico City, and Hockney discovered a hotel with a courtyard which fascinated him and to which he was anxious to return. Just as Tyler had pre-viously developed a lithographic method allowing maximum spontaneity for Oldenburg's *Notes*, so he now offered Hockney a range of coloured crayons and paints suitable for use on sheets of transparent Mylar plastic. These transparent sheets functioned as ready-made colour separations for Hockney to overlay, one above the other, so that he could visualize the completed picture as he went along.

plate 98

88 Ken Tyler, Lee Funderburg and Roger Campbell helping the artist Ed Baynard to print one of his woodcuts in 1980

89 Richard Hamilton: *Flowerpiece B, cyan separation*, 1975, 25½ x 19¾ in (64.7 x 50.1 cm), lithograph, edition 23

90,91,92 Work at Tyler Graphics on the Michael Heizer project of 1976

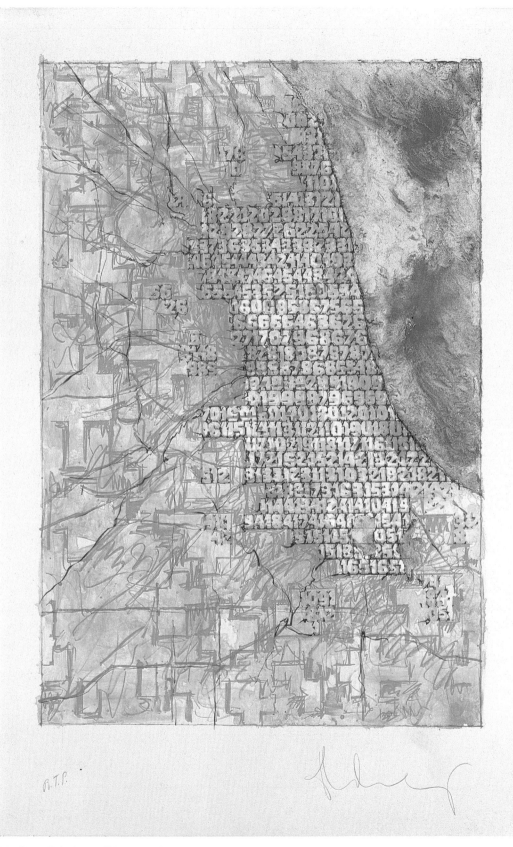

93 Claes Oldenburg, *Chicago stuffed with numbers*, 1976, 47½ x 31¼ in (120.6 x 79.3 cm), lithograph, edition 85

94 Roy Lichtenstein: *American Indian theme VI*, 1979, 37½ X 50¼ in (95.2 x 127.6 cm), woodcut, edition 50

95 Ken Tyler working on Oldenburg's *Chicago stuffed with numbers*

96 Tyler and Oldenburg with a proof of *Chicago stuffed with numbers*, 1976

97   Roy Lichtenstein: *Goldfish bowl*, 1981, 25 x 18 in (63.5 x 45.7 cm), woodcut, edition 30

98   A trial proof of *Hotel, Acatlan: second day*, from the lithographic project worked on by David Hockney early in 1985

The same drawings were then used to obtain the printing surface on the lithographic plates. This new procedure reduced working time and the tedious delays in proofing which had made Hockney reluctant to do much colour printing in the past. With the new system, Tyler was able to produce in a day what would previously have taken a week. By June 1985, when he gave a lecture at the Canberra School of Art[3] during a visit to Australia, Tyler announced that since he had begun working with Hockney the artist had made 527 plates, using 600 colours, and that before the end of the year they expected to complete a cycle of some 40 prints. Moreover, the refrigerated bed of his lithographic press allowed Tyler to preserve the most delicate and tenuous washes.

plates 102-103

The system of lithographic transfer from a transparent drawing surface, such as glass, plastic or various types of film, was first used for map-making in pre-war Germany and then spread to Holland and England, where W. S. Cowell of Ipswich developed it as an autolithographic process.[4] Immediately after the second world war, an adventurous businesswoman who was pioneering these materials persuaded Picasso, Braque and other famous European artists to draw a set of prints for school children.[5] Subsequently, Henry Moore, who had been included in the school print portfolio, made great use of the process in his work at the Curwen Studio.

Tyler's innovation consisted in making it possible for Hockney to draw in colour on these plastic sheets. He had tried it out already with Malcolm Morley, Joan Mitchell and Motherwell and had a solid basis of work experience which allowed him to refine

plates 99-100

99 Malcolm Morley:
Beach scene, 1982, 38 x
51½ in (96.5 x 130.8 cm),
lithograph, edition 58

100 Malcolm Morley:
Goats in shed, 28½ x 40½
in (72.3 x 102.8 cm),
lithograph, edition 30

101   David Hockney's colour litho project in the artist's studio at Tyler Graphics workshop, January 1985

102,103   David Hockney and Ken Tyler working at the Tyler Graphics studio in January 1985

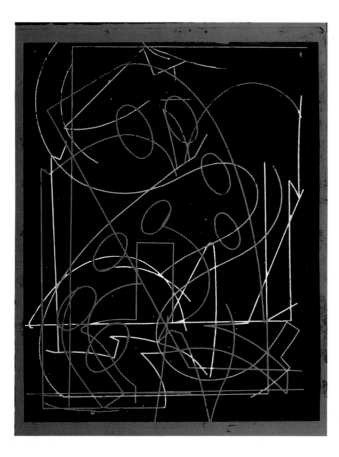

104 Frank Stella: *Talladega Five I*, 1982, 66¼ x 51¼ (168.2 x 130.1 cm), relief etching, woodcut, edition 30

105 Frank Stella: *Imola Three IV*, 1982, 66 x 52 in (167.6 x 132.0 cm), relief etching, screenprint on dyed paper, edition 30

106 Frank Stella: *Estoril Five I*, 1982, 66¼ x 51½ in (168.2 x 130.8 cm), relief etching, woodcut on dyed paper, edition 30

it further for Hockney's benefit. Enthusiastic about the first proofs of Hockney's work pulled early in 1985, Tyler was predicting that his adaptation of the process would open up a new chapter in colour printing. He was also delighted with an ingenious adaptation of the magnesium plates he and Stella had discovered, which he had etched with linen, sandpaper and other textured surfaces so that Hockney could place them under the Mylar when he was drawing. This enabled the artist to achieve effects similar to those derived by Fantin-Latour, Whistler and Braque, among others, by drawing on transfer paper placed over textural book linens. By superimposing three blues drawn in such a way, Hockney could obtain a colour mezzotint quality which Tyler believed was 'a great, great advance' and one which 'turned the artist on to

plate 101   color'.[6]

In this new body of work, Hockney has moved on from the discoveries he has made in photography and is trying to develop a new way of seeing, informed by Chinese painting while at the same time moving on from Cubism. The artist is convinced that one-point perspective, which is the basis of ninety-eight percent of the images we produce — whether in painting, photography, film or on television — is actually a distorted way of looking at the world. He hopes that by combining many perspectives and points of view, and by softening the edges of his pictures by extending colour onto the frames, he will emphasize the relativity of vision. He wants to debunk the western idea that the world should be represented from the point of view of a stationary viewer with one eye closed. This notion, he feels, has resulted not only in the illusion that there is such a thing as objectivity, but in the perception that the infinite is always 'a very long way away'. His strategy, then, is to present many perspectives simultaneously and, by forcing the eye to move over the surface, to encourage the viewer to become part of the picture, rather than separate (and alienated) from it.

He believes that he returned to Tyler Graphics to make more prints at just the right moment, for the technique Tyler had refined for his use was perfect for what he wanted to say. For Hockney, the difference between Tyler and most other printers was his constant invention. Moreover, he loved colour and was therefore constantly researching new inks and providing options of which another printer might not be aware. 'With Ken you get a collaborator', Hockney said, but added:

> Frankly you don't always. He makes me keep at it in the best possible way. I might think: 'It's a mess . . . I'll give up'. But that's where Ken comes in and you know it's going to be possible. He keeps you at it and then the endless struggle is worth it . . . He's willing to chuck prints away. That's very important, because that gives you a little more freedom . . . you can take a lot more risks. Real collaborators are quite rare actually. Because a collaborator is offering you something and then you offer him something back. And with somebody like Ken, what he's offering you is something you couldn't do on your own — something you don't even know about . . . I think all my best prints have been made here.[7]

One of the greatest achievements to date in Tyler's collaborative life was realized in the early 1980s when he worked for a protracted period with Frank Stella. Between

plates 104-106   1980 and 1983, artist and printer produced two major series, the *Circuits* and the
plates 107-108   *Swan engravings*. These prints kept Tyler's workshop busy almost non-stop for the entire period. The *Swan engravings* are black and white etchings made of hand-drawn magnesium plates collaged together with 'found' fragments of the same material once used to emboss lace-patterned plastic tablecloths. The *Circuits* are large-scale richly coloured images made by the sophisticated use of both the relief and intaglio surfaces of wood and metal, in some cases printed on custom-made Tyler Graphics paper consisting of myriad multicoloured patches. Both suites are simultaneous by-products of Stella's *Circuit* paintings.

A journalist said of Stella that between the 1960s and the 1980s he travelled the entire stylistic spectrum from 'a rarified purism to intuitive expressionism'. There is certainly a vast difference between the austere-shaped black stripe paintings with which he originally made his name and the recent dynamic, almost baroque reliefs that

107 Frank Stella: *Swan engraving III*, 1981/82, 66 x 52 in (167.6 x 132.0 cm), intaglio and relief etching, edition 30

108 Frank Stella: *Swan engraving blue*, 1982/83, 38 x 31½ in (96.5 x 80.0 cm), relief etching, engraving, woodcut, edition 30

109 Frank Stella: *Puerto Rican blue pigeon* from the *Exotic bird* series, 1977, 34 x 46 in (86.3 x 116.8 cm), offset lithograph, screenprint with glitter, edition 50

employ honeycomb structures with skins of etched metal scribbled with frenetically lacy colour. Stella's early work is often described as detached and impersonal, the more recent production as fervent and spontaneous. Robert Rosenblum, however, who wrote the first monograph about the painter,[8] warned that to pigeon-hole Stella as 'cool' was naive. The paintings, he said, were charged with 'intensely personal energies that are all the more potent for being so rigorously disciplined' and he described them in terms of 'velocities of pictorial highways' that one was forced to follow as if behind the wheel of a speeding car.[9] This same description could do service for Stella's most recent works, in which energetic serpentine curves wriggle and bend with dizzying speed — in paintings actually named after car-racing circuits.

Stella had taken a rest from printmaking between 1974 and 1977, although he worked with Tyler on his paper constructions during that period. When he eventually returned to graphic art at Bedford Village, it was to combine screenprinting and lithography more thoroughly than before, employing liquid tusche rather than crayoning and christening the offset press Tyler had installed. The artist said:

> The *Eccentric polygons* got me started . . . they weren't that great, I had hoped for better than the end result. Still once I had gotten started in a more expansive direction, once I had a feel for the possibility of making prints that were like what I wanted to do in painting, things began to happen. The *Polygons* paved the way for the *Exotic birds* . . .
>
> . . . In the end, it was the flatbed offset press that set me free. I could roll the image over the paper the way I could brush paint over a surface.[10]

The exuberant *Exotic bird series*, which were Tyler's first editioned offset lithographs from Bedford Village, rioted with French Curves and sparkled with applied glitter. The scribbled crayoning Stella had used for the *Eccentric polygons*, which were made just before Tyler left Los Angeles, became even more wild and free and thin films of lithographic colour were played off against the thicker chalkier deposits of screenprinting ink.

plate 109

Although he worked again at the Petersburg Press (on a series dedicated to a racing driver friend killed in the Grand Prix at Monza), Stella told the cataloguer of his prints that Tyler had taught him everything he knew about printing:

He probably still does. He knows so much. It's a nice thing. He tells me how it's done. I say, 'Can we do it this way?'. And he sees if it can be done, or approximates it, or has a better idea. We keep working away at it. I don't know enough to get it myself.[11]

In the period between completion of his last graphic suite with Tyler on the west coast and the first one made in the east, Stella began to see that the techniques and materials of printmaking could be used for his relief paintings in metal. The scribbling with lithographic crayon seen in the *Eccentric polygons* was used on the aluminium surfaces of his *Brazilian* reliefs to form a resist or protection against etching with caustic. The purpose of the etching was to roughen the metal sufficiently to allow it to accept colouring by screenprinting ink, magna and oil stick. This interplay between techniques of printing and painting changed Stella's attitude to printmaking and 'things opened up'.

While he was etching the *Brazilian* paintings, it was suggested to Stella that magnesium would be a superior surface to aluminium. The introduction to the scale and fidelity of the new metal at the Swan Engraving Co. proved to be as liberating to the artist as his introduction to offset. When one saw areas of twelve square feet of magnesium in the huge commercial vats, said Stella, one 'didn't need to be a genius to see that they would make dynamite prints'.[12] Tyler and the artist took some of the etched magnesium back to Bedford Village.

> Everyone thinks a project just takes off, that it's like magic. But they looked awful. So for six or eight months the plates just sat around, until we started working on them again. I don't know when the turning-point came. I guess we saw the laser drawings, the tracings left on the wood by the laser's routing. We inked one of those up and the drawing looked so spectacular that it got me started. Things started falling into place and began to take off.[13]

Whereas he had previously painted with printmaking techniques, now Stella said he tried 'to make prints about printing. These prints are painterly, but they are painterly in the way that printing can be, not in the way that painting is painterly'.[14]

In the early days, Stella would take an image to proof stage and would then leave the press to do the editioning. Nowadays his working method is very different. He keeps working on the prints, making various states,[15] some of which are editioned. As he himself puts it: 'I keep working on the plates as we go along and we proof and run. We don't know what it is going to look like until we get to the last run'.[16]

A fellow printer, Jack Lemon of Landfall Press, has described the relationship between Stella and Tyler as 'like a marriage',[17] with each able to read the other's mind. Clinton Adams points out that there is no way Stella could have made the *Circuit* and *Swan engraving* series without Tyler's help.[18] Stella confirms that he can 'only go as far as the printers can. If they don't have the energy, if they hang back, I can't carry it'. He adds:

> Well the printer is sort of everything in one sense. If you can't get along and you can't agree — if you're not doing it together — then there's no point in doing it, it doesn't work. You have to create a level of excitement to keep the project going, and if they're not into it and if you can't turn each other on, then it really doesn't work so good, it's no fun actually.[19]

He confirms Tyler's openness and willingness to try anything:

> I do whatever I want there and I notice most of the other artists who work there do pretty much whatever they please too . . . With Ken, he pretty much goes along. I say: 'Gee, that looks great', and he says: 'Yes, that will be great' and we just figure out a way to do it. We don't say our press isn't big enough, we go find a press where we can do it. Or if we have to, we drive a truck over it . . .[20]

Stella describes the elaboration of new techniques and processes as 'jumping from puddle to puddle . . . you develop the technical expertise after you've done it'.[21]

The understanding between the two men is such that Tyler, who remarks that Stella's ego 'is not fragile', says the artist often allows him to:

> . . . embellish the print surface by suggesting additional color printings. He doesn't discount

110 Frank Stella and Ken Tyler preparing magnesium plates for the *Swan engraving* series

it as useless interference. I think it's a positive attitude. I'm always running off with the artist's work, trying another inking to see if it can be richer or more successful this way or that way if a process is altered. The artist accepts that is part of the thing they get when they come to work with me. It can be a pain in the neck at times, but most of the time it produces results.[22]

Tyler believes his job is to generate excitement and to make the artist, 'who's on "Candid Camera" ', as comfortable as possible. Creating the right setting and atmosphere is the theatrical part of the job. What he wanted '. . . was for artists to make statements that were much more generous and much more open-ended and more expansive so that the craft could have a bigger horizon line . . .'[23]

Stella feels that there were three 'giant technical changes'[24] that helped liberate his printmaking — offset, etched magnesium and papermaking. He did not know why in the past he had accepted the limitations of commercial paper.[25] Because of the difficulties of printing metal engravings with multiple runs,[26] Tyler had suggested putting colour into the paper first, because the special sheets composed of multicoloured patches made one transparent colour printed over them take on myriad hues. At a seminar, Tyler, with 'justifiable pride',[27] revealed the special crane and winch he had rigged up to lift the heavy sheets of wet pulp from the vat. These sheets exceeded in size anything he had done before. Stella described the suites he made at Tyler Graphics as:

. . the best simply because they're printing at its best. There are two kinds of printing — we've done some really good color printing too. We've done some fifty or sixty prints that hold up pretty well. We've done some very good layered printing, which is layer on layer on layer and made it quite beautiful and made it literally quite painterly. I mean as painterly as paintings get. But I'm not proud of that, although it is technically more sophisticated than most of the things. But I like the black and white prints because they have the power of printing, the thing that printing does best, which is to make an impression. To hit it just once with black ink on white paper is really the ultimate thrill.[28]

The fantastic input and commitment on the part of the printer is illustrated by the fact that a single print from one of the smallest *Swan engravings* took the best part of a day to hand-wipe. Tyler said of this:

plates 107-108

Frank knows what Rodney goes through to wipe those etching plates. He's there, he sees him all day long wiping his plate. Frank knows that, he knows the labor that's gone into that. He knows that Rodney doesn't give up, he knows that his hands are doing it the same way every day and sometimes his hands hurt. And when he comes over and says thank you, it's simple, but you know it's thank you.[29]

Stella's suites have received widespread and unanimous critical acclaim. Clifford Ackley, of the Boston Museum of Fine Arts, wrote of them as a 'creative breakthrough' that would have been 'impossible without the high-tech wizardry and inventiveness of the printer'. They were virtuoso prints, he said, that 'transcended mere virtuosity'. Their 'visual heft and punch' accounted for the frequent comment that the installation looked 'like a painting show rather than a print show'. Ackley continued: 'The prints have their own independence and integrity, a rich new materiality and physicality of surface conceived strictly in terms of the properties of the printed image and the fabric of the paper itself'.[30]

Barry Walker applauded Stella's transition from 'an artist who also made prints to, in the most profound sense, an artist printmaker'.[31]

The critic Robert Hughes, describing the *Swan engravings* as 'one of the most brilliant and audacious suites of black and white prints produced recently, or indeed ever', went on:

> No modern artist since Picasso in the forties has given us black and white prints of this opulence and strength, and not even he worked at this size . . . With the *Swan engravings* Stella finally becomes as important to printing as he is to painting.[32]

Stella, who said he 'got more into printing than I ever intended', believes himself that the *Swan engravings* were 'as good as anything anyone had ever printed' — an opinion which, even if it was a vain delusion, he held 'with firm conviction'.[33] Tyler for his part believed that the artist:

> . . . had made some of the greatest black and white etchings of all time. I think Dürer would absolutely walk over here and tip his hat . . . I think they're as good as anything Dürer ever did and I hold Dürer in great esteem . . .
>
> The surface on those prints would have been impossible in 1960, totally impossible. There wasn't enough known, there wasn't enough freedom and certainly Frank in 1960 wouldn't have put the kind of creative energy into a print project. And we wouldn't have been able to have the privilege of making all those trials and errors to get there . . .
>
> This compulsive effort to push for another dimension does in the end create prints of greater quality, providing there's a good image somewhere within the layers of ink, paper, techniques and personalities.[34]

TYLER'S ACHIEVEMENT

The retail cost of thirty thousand U.S. dollars for the largest of Stella's recent *Circuit* images, *Pergusa three double*, has worried a number of people, including Tyler him- plate 111 self. While the price is commensurate with the cost of Stella's unique works in the market and with the amount of time and money that has been invested in the prints, Tyler knows that the juggernaut has to slow down.

> The prints are getting too expensive . . . this thing is going to blow itself up eventually. We're not going to be making $30,000 Stellas every day. This is very unusual and I think it's probably the very last time you're going to see it. I think we have to return to a little smaller scale because we just can't do this kind of thing for every artist coming through here.[1]

Stella for his part is tired of hearing that the prices for his prints are too high:

> In the last four years, every time I've brought one out, they say I've made too many and they're too expensive. I get tired of hearing about it. They should buy cheaper prints by someone else.[2]

When you multiply the price by the edition size, says Stella, it sounds like a fantastic amount of money —

> . . . but the other side of the coin is that two and a half years of a shop working full time on one project with four or five printers is into the hundreds and hundreds of thousands of dollars . . . I don't care. All I'm going to lose is my time and some money, but we invest sometimes high time and money into a project so that a printer's whole shop could be at risk. If it were an unsuccessful project after printing two and a half years with it he could pretty much go out of business and then it would be my fault . . . It takes a little bit of the fun out of it.[3]

For Tyler, risk is necessary 'if you're going to change and grow'. He has consistently refused to indulge in cost analysis and considered the very notion 'bananasville' when it was suggested at Tamarind. He believes that a project costs what it costs and that the printer has to see it through regardless: 'To this day, I have refused to let any accountant tell me to break these things down into categories or tell me that there has to be a ceiling . . .'[4]

Despite the accusation sometimes made that Tyler runs 'a money press', he has always spent a high proportion of the press's time on research and development and the dangers involved have been enormous:

> I can burn up $100,000 so fast it will make your head spin. And that's a little tiny place I work in. I'm not General Motors, but it's like a conduit to the dumpster . . . You know I've had to borrow vast sums of money and it was nip and tuck and I was about ready to fold up the tent and say quit.[5]

While he can only enter into a really extensive collaboration with an artist of Stella's popularity for such an investment to be feasible, Tyler likes the fact that he can pass on the discoveries and technical possibilities to a younger artist, as has happened recently in the case of the Minneapolis artist Steve Sorman, who thinks graphically with instinct and freedom:

> After those beautiful Stellas it's a wonderful joy to see a young artist like Steve Sorman come here, pick up on that and take it a little bit further. The new Sormans are smashing prints and I'm very, very proud of them. I think they reach a new height in mixed-media printmaking. It's a building block situation. I love it and when I see it, I'm very, very pleased.[6] plates 114-115

Thus, the rather simplistic and problematic philosophy, enunciated by W. S. Lieberman, that 'great artists make great prints' (which never really sorted out how one might distinguish the great from the merely fashionable, or encourage those who

111 Frank Stella: *Pergusa Three Double*, 1984, 101½ x 66 in (257.9 x 167.6 cm), relief etching, engraving, screenprint on two sheets, edition 30

112 Steve Sorman hand painting one of his monotypes, summer 1984

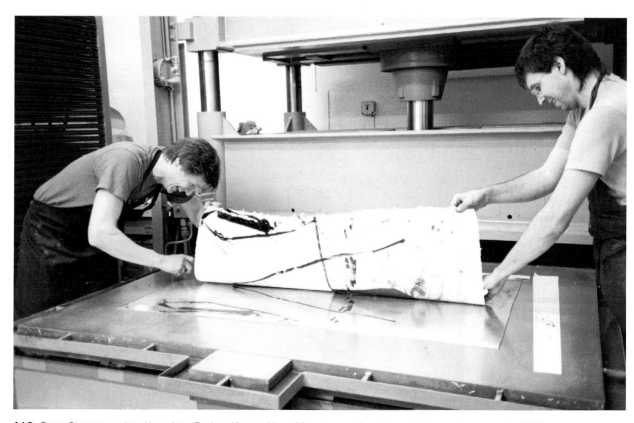

113 Steve Sorman, assisted by printer Rodney Konopaki, working on a section of one of his monotypes, spring 1984

had not yet made international reputations) has been modified to admit the promising and up-and-coming artist as well.

Tyler knows that he is what he is because of the artists he chose to work with. He also knows that while the single, traditional and essentially drawn prints are made in much the same way as they always were, his role in the production of complicated mixed-media prints, ambitious large-scale prints and prints which pioneer innovative and experimental processes for the first time, has developed into something quite new in printmaking.

Although he earned the title by covering the requisite ground at Tamarind, he has never really considered himself a master printer:

> I like to be called a collaborator. I think I'm learning. I don't think I'm a master yet, but in order to do good work, you need an ego. You have to have it, or you get so bruised you can't do anything. You've got to be stubborn to do good art and you've got to be stubborn to do good printing.[7]

Tyler is a collaborator first and a publisher second, for he believes the art must always come first. He himself works all hours and seven days a week:

> There's a madness to what I do, putting that kind of pressure on myself, having a seven-day week for periods of time . . . You're a little more sensitive to everything and the art starts to talk back and it gets into you and everything is cross-pollinating and you have a much more generous atmosphere and the shop flows . . . When you put it on a strict short week and you start to get very choosy about what you're going to do because it takes too much time — well, you can't make the kind of prints that I make in that situation.[8]

In all the hype and super-hype that has attended him since he began his first shop in California, the real clue to understanding Tyler has been largely overlooked. It is simply that he is a maker. Whenever he talks about printing he is absolutely consistent in his enthusiasm. He became a printer in the first place because he was never happier than when he was using his hands. In 1983 he confirmed that:

> Being on a one-to-one basis with that press and that work. It's the one thing that's going to stand up, the one-to-one . . . And the printer today still has the best opportunity for the most enjoyment in this business. I really feel that if you're a printer, you're a printer and that's a terrific thing to be and you should put all your energies into that.[9]

And in 1984 he added, 'I just like to do it. I get caught up in the rhythm . . . I really like it'.[10]

Pinned to Tyler's notice board is a saying from Norman Mailer that 'In this time of immense distraction, anyone who can truly exercise craft is to be admired'. He believes in the importance of creative energy and he wants his own to 'get a little bit better as I go along'. It is interesting to note that when Stella was asked if he wanted to be known as a printmaker, he said he did not because he felt it was 'a little tacky'. 'However', he added, 'to be a printer is a worthwhile activity. I wouldn't mind being a printer'.[11]

Despite all the rubbish that has passed for criticism on the subject of Tyler's house style, and while his prints still have the flawless California finish when required, he considers that clear lush washes and clean bright colours have been his most distinctive contribution. What he believes he has achieved at Bedford Village is an understanding of surface that is 'rarely found in modern printmaking'. He spends considerable time poring over the history of prints to find out whether there's anything that he can use again — 'I don't know if I've invented much, but I've certainly reinvented quite a bit'.[12]

One could interpret Tyler's various printer's chops in terms of an unconscious symbolism. The first, from Tamarind, which resembles a Volkswagen or a beetle, shows the printer's initials as an arrow pushing ahead; the second, from Gemini, shows two figures and a containing wall; while the third, for his present shop, consists of two sheets, floating free. Tyler Graphics, he says, is:

> . . . a little place giving lots of opportunities, making a lot of things available that weren't

114 Steve Sorman: *From outside (inside)*, 1984, 97 x 43 in (246.3 x 109.2 cm), monotype etching, woodcut, collage, with hand painting

115 Steve Sorman: *Still standing still*, 1984, 66¼ x 43 in (168.2 x 109.2 cm),
lithograph, woodcut, linecut, collage, hand painting, edition 20

available years before. I think we've done a lot to dispel these goddamned rules that have buggered people up so badly . . . Print no longer has all these little restrictions. It's been opened up . . .[13]

Tyler's teacher, Garo Antreasian, believes that 'the lasting power to do this very difficult work is something that is of great significance'.[14] Tyler says the job gets easier after a while — 'you can say to yourself: "I've really accomplished something" '.[15] For two decades now, he has been tenaciously balancing tradition and innovation, sound business practice and the risks of research and development with some success, and he is perhaps a little more relaxed about what he has achieved.

I think the quiet satisfaction within me these days is my knowledge that you cannot separate my role in the prints made in my workshop. Whatever contribution I've made, with whatever innovation, is for me clearly a part of the graphic work. The prints have my hand in them and I think that's a good thing. If the work is not successful as art, then my hand in it is of no value.[16]

And he adds:

In this society, there is a tendency to idolize a man's life-style instead of the work he does. In the end, just look at my work. I think I'll stand behind that.[17]

ACKNOWLEDGEMENTS

No book is made without abundant help from many people and this one, written in double-quick time, is no exception. It would not have been possible at all without the wholehearted support of Ken Tyler himself, who supplied much documentary material.

I am also indebted to colleagues at the Australian National Gallery who made useful editorial comment — among them Alan Dodge, Lanier Graham, Alistair Hay, Terence Measham, Sharon Sullivan and Ross Woodrow — while Dana Rowan brought a high level of painstaking care to the editing of the manuscript and subsequent proofreading.

The founder, present Director and first master printer of Tamarind — June Wayne, Clinton Adams and Garo Antreasian — were kind enough to advise on the section dealing with that institution and the distinguished American print curators, Ruth Fine and Riva Castleman, provided most useful help and comment.

The curatorial assistants of the International Print Department — Cathy Leahy and Stephen Coppel — who worked on the Australian National Gallery's exhibition, *Ken Tyler : Printer Extraordinary*, supervised the photography of prints in the collection and Cathy prepared the appendix listing unique works related to the Tyler archive owned by the Australian people.

Lanier Graham drafted the short chronology of Tyler's career and was the principal architect of the bibliography, which was typed from my initial listing by the International Print Department's secretary, Margaret Stack.

Bruce Moore, Matt Kelso and Erwin Potas, photographers to the Australian National Gallery, provided those illustrations stemming from its collection and Jessie Birch gave indispensable help in preparing the photography for publication.

My thanks are also due to the staff of the Royal Canberra Hospital who made it possible for me to keep writing to schedule during an unexpected sojourn.

Last, but not least, gratitude to Alex and Alexandra who know what such work costs, but whose support is always total.

Photo credits

Ken Tyler of Tyler Graphics 1, 10, 11, 12, 13, 15, 21, 23, 29, 30, 32, 33, 36, 37, 38, 41, 44, 54, 56, 57, 59, 61, 62, 63, 64, 65, 66, 67, 70, 72, 73, 74, 75, 76, 77, 78, 79, 80, 85, 86, 88, 89, 90, 91, 92, 94, 95, 96, 98, 99, 100, 101, 102, 103, 104, 105, 106, 110, 111, 112, 113, 114, 115.
Curwen Studio 5.
Gemini G.E.L. 2, 3.
Pat Gilmour 34, 58.
Universal Limited Art Editions 7, 8.
Australian National Gallery *Frontispiece,* 13, 17, 19, 20, 21, 22, 24, 25, 27, 28, 35, 36, 37, 38, 39, 42, 43, 45, 46, 47, 48, 49, 50, 51, 52, 53, 55, 71, 81, 83, 84, 93, 97, 107, 108, 109.
Individual photographers:
Hans Namuth 60; Robert Petersen 7; Herbert Matter 8; Betty Fiske 10; Kay Tyler 16, 112, 113; William Crutchfield 13; Malcolm Lubliner 29, 30, 54; Steve Sloman 64, 65; Jill Richards 72, 74; Lindsay Green 85, 86, 88, 110.

KENNETH E. TYLER—
A CHRONOLOGY

1931	Born in East Chicago, Indiana, December 13
1950–51	Studied at Art Institute of Chicago
1951–52	Attended Indiana University
1952–54	Joined U.S. Army Corps of Engineers
1954–57	Attended University of Chicago (part-time), Art Institute of Chicago (full-time) and graduated with a Bachelor of Art Education degree from the Art Institute of Chicago
1957	Invented and patented a Riser Scaffold Unit
1962–63	Studied lithography with Garo Antreasian and graduated with a Master of Art Education degree from John Herron School of Art, Indianapolis
1963	Received Ford Foundation Grant to study printing at Tamarind Lithography Workshop in Los Angeles
	During August, studied with Marcel Durassier, Parisian master printer, and visitor to Tamarind
1964–65	Technical Director of Tamarind Lithography Workshop, Los Angeles
1965	Designed first of several hydraulic lithographic presses
	Formed GEMINI Ltd., Los Angeles, with Kay Tyler, in July
1966	Formed GEMINI G.E.L., Los Angeles, with Sidney Felsen and Stanley Grinstein, in February
	Exhibition of Albers' *White line squares* at Los Angeles County Museum of Art
1967	Received grant from National

	Endowment for the Arts for research and development of paper, embossing and three-dimensional works
1970	Exhibitions of Gemini prints at the De Young Museum in San Francisco and the Los Angeles County Museum of Art
	Featured in *Life* magazine
1971	Major exhibition of Gemini editions at the Museum of Modern Art in New York: 'Technics and Creativity: Gemini G.E.L.'
	Featured in *Time* magazine
1973	Ken Tyler's collection of approximately 600 printer's proofs plus preparatory works bought by the Australian National Gallery, Canberra
1974	Formed TYLER WORKSHOP Ltd., Bedford Village, New York
1975	Formed TYLER GRAPHICS Ltd., Bedford Village, New York
1978	Patented invention of Tycore, a system of rigid structuring for paper
1981	GEMINI G.E.L. Archive established at the National Gallery of Art, Washington, D.C.
1984	Major exhibition of GEMINI G.E.L. editions at National Gallery of Art, Washington, D.C.: 'GEMINI G.E.L.: Art and Collaboration'
	Tyler Graphics Archive opens in Walker Art Center, Minneapolis, 21 September 1984
1985	Major exhibition at Australian National Gallery, Canberra: 'Ken Tyler: Printer Extraordinary'

NOTES

Introduction

1. June Wayne quoted in DONSON, B.39, p.189.

2. GOLDMAN, B.62, p.62.

3. HUGHES, A.19, p.56.

4. Judith Goldman, 'Twenty-Five Years of American Prints and Printmaking, 1956–1981', in STASIK, ed., C.65, p.12.

5. Rubens was both painter and diplomat and excelled at publicizing his own work. See DONSON, B.39, p.218.

6. FINE, A.10, p.39: 'From the shop's beginning, its spirit has been based on the premise that anything is possible.'

7. *Life*, C.49, p.57.

8. Josef Albers in 'Synopsis', from BUCHER, B.21, p.10.

9. Clinton Adams and June Wayne, although interviewed separately, made almost identical statements about Tyler and Albers on 26 and 30 September 1983 respectively (ADAMS, D.1 and WAYNE, D.32).

10. DONSON, B.39, p.220.

11. Maurice Tuchman quoted in ISENBERG, C.40.

12. See KRAMER, A.22.

13. FINE observes that Jasper Johns and Roy Lichtenstein 'both produced series of prints that have become monuments in the history of American graphic art'. See A.10, p.39.

14. The printer/curator Timothy Isham in conversation with Ruth FINE, 7 April 1983. See A.10, pp.20,32. 'Wizard' is a word continually used in reference to Tyler.

15. As well as holding the R.T.P. (right-to-print) proofs of almost all the Gemini G.E.L. editions up to 1973, the Australian National Gallery owns preparatory drawings and rare proofs etc. which are listed in the appendix, pp. 155-156.

16. See note 4 above.

17. David Hockney in STANGOS, ed., B.106, p.100.

18. Frank Stella interviewed by Judith GOLDMAN in B.64, p.13.

19. LANGSNER, C.43, p.34.

20. Robert Motherwell at the dedication of the Walker Art Center, Minneapolis, 21 September 1984.

The background to Tyler's career and the 'print renaissance'

Lithography in America

1. For the full story of the Curwen Press, see GILMOUR, B.56.

2. CATE, B.26.

3. ADAMS, B.1, p.5.

4. Janson was writing an introduction to Emil Ganso, *The Technique of Lithographic Printing* (1940), and is quoted in ADAMS, B.1, p.159.

5. SHERRILL, A.42, pp.54, 55.

6. *Time*, C.46.

7. KASE, B.77, p.96.

8. CRICHTON, B.34, p.44.

9. In 1971, while preparing his book *Jasper Johns*, Crichton had long discussions with Tyler. See TYLER, D.28.

10. Ben Berns interview transcript in TERENZIO, rev. ed., B.107, p.41.

11. *Print Collector's Newsletter*, A.33, p.5.

12. ANTREASIAN, C.4, p.184.

13. MOURLOT, B.90, p.93 and cat. nos 64 and 65, *Pigeon on a grey background* and *White pigeon on a black background*, 1 and 4 February 1947. Mourlot wrote: 'From time to time he [Picasso] would visit his friends at Rue de Chabrol and thank Raymond Tutin, the pressman who worked for him and who often cursed his lithographic oddities'.

The implications of changing styles for graphic art

1. Oscar Schlemmer quoted in WILLETT, B.119, p.81.

2. Reprint of Louis Lozowick's article from *Machine Age Exposition* (1927), in FLINT, B.47, pp.18,19.

3. The term 'plastic' is used here in the sense of shaping or forming the materials of art.

4. See WILLIAMS, B.121, pp.167–169, for an interesting discussion of the term 'mechanical'.

5. JANSON/JANSON, B.70, p.11.

6. RENÉ, C.54, p.193.

7. As above, p.194.

8. ROSE, B.98, p.21: 'It seems probable that the

central experience in the changing structure, in fact, his discovery of the all over linear configuration — the philosophy of risk underlying it and all of Pollock's subsequent work — is in the automatism of the printmaking.'

9. S. W. Hayter interviewed by Pat Gilmour in STASIK, ed., C.66, pp.11-18.

10. TERENZIO, B.107, p.44.

11. Information given by Gabor Peterdi, interviewed by Judith Goldman, in STASIK, ed., C.66, pp.6-10.

12. 'Five Degrees of Originality in Printmaking' in HAYTER, B.67, pp.123-135.

13. HOLLANDER, D.17.

14. *Print Collector's Newsletter*, A.33, p.5.

15. HESS, C.37, p.29.

Universal Limited Art Editions

1. Quoted by Sam Wagstaff who published screenprints by ten American painters in 1964. See WAGSTAFF, D.31.

2. RIVERS, C.55, p.101.

3. GRAY, C.35, p.84.

4. TOMKINS, C.68, p.54.

5. The book in question was Monroe Wheeler, *Modern Painters and Sculptors as Illustrators* (New York: Museum of Modern Art, 1936).

6. RIVERS, C.55, p.102.

7. TOMKINS, C.68, p.44.

8. GOLDSTON, D.15.

9. PHILLIPS, C.50, p.102.

10. TOMKINS, C.68, p.66.

11. YOUNG, C.76, p.52.

12. RIVERS, C.55, p.102.

13. LIEBERMAN, D.20.

14. Tatyana Grosman interview transcript in TERENZIO, B.107, p.52.

15. RIVERS, C.55, p.102.

16. WAGSTAFF, D.31.

17. TOMKINS, C.68, p.84.

18. Essay by Robert Motherwell, 'The Book's Beginnings', dated 22 September 1972, in McHENDRY, B.87, n.p.

19. Statement made during the dedication of new building, including Tyler Archive, at Walker Art Center, Minneapolis, on 21 September 1984.

20. Statement made in conversation with Thelma KASE on 11 March 1972: 'The artists who do prints with other publishers come back bringing new challenges and experiences. It is beneficial to all concerned.' See KASE, B.77.

21. HOLLANDER, D.17.

22. Richard FIELD (B.44, p.2) says: 'Having come from France the Grosmans naturally turned to lithography rather than other print media. The Parisian ateliers had provided the model'; James SCHUYLER (C.60, p.36) notes that 'A long residence in Paris may explain, in some measure, why the lithographs published by her [Tanya Grosman] are as svelte and finished as those of Picasso and Miro'; Elizabeth ARMSTRONG (A.1, p.8) says: 'She brought with her a lofty view of the potential of lithography'. Yet Thelma KASE said of Mrs Grosman after interviewing her: 'She simply maintains that she had no direct contact with lithography, only an awareness of artists'. In fact the first prints the Grosmans produced in America were screenprinted reproductions (see B.77).

23. Important new information about the way the German Expressionists printed their lithographs can be found in a statement made by Erich Heckel to Roman Norbert Ketterer on 24 October 1958. See CAREY/GRIFFITHS, B.22, pp.37-39.

24. Tanya Grosman quoted in TERENZIO, B.107, p.53 — 'I leave the artists very much alone'.

25. CASTLEMAN, C.14.

26. JONES, C.41, p.14.

27. Thelma KASE interviewed both Zigmunds Priede (June 1972) and Bill Goldston (March 1972) and observed that: 'Goldstone [*sic*] and Priede emphasized the tremendous frustration of having to sublimate one's own creative instincts to those of the artist. The printer must fit himself to the artist, be his slave, his extension, his second set of arms. It is this which is most difficult for the printer to accomplish. Particularly because he is an artist too. As a printer with an artist's background, he can be sensitive to the artist's needs, but he also need [*sic*] an outlet for his own artistic expression. This is what finally made Priede leave U.L.A.E., although he does return every summer. Goldstone [*sic*] continues to paint in his hours away from the workshop, and he has no intention of making printing his life's work'. See KASE, B.77.

28. GOLDSTON, D.15.

29. Ben Berns quoted in TERENZIO, B.107, p.49 — 'They had a new artist every month. It didn't seem very interesting to me, so I didn't take the job. The situation was entirely different at West Islip. It struck me first as though somebody had found a press and opened a shop in a garage . . . which in fact was the case!'.

30. TOMKINS, C.69, p.84.

31. FIELD, B.44: 'It is a guarded secret that at least one extra little image was required to patch up the table during the printing . . .' Johns asked for the same stone to be used throughout and for one numeral to be erased as the next was added. This introduced the difficulty of continually 'opening' and 'closing' the printing matrix without getting what one printer has called 'duck soup'.

32. TOMKINS, C.68, p.65.

33. RIVERS, C.55, p.102.

34. TOMKINS, C.68, p.76.

Tamarind Lithography Workshop
1. RODMAN, B.96 (interview with June Wayne): 'She has carried the lithograph both technically and communicatively further than her painting.'

2. The plan was 'To restore the art of the lithograph in the United States'. Briefly, the six points — given fully in GEDEON, B.52, p.11 — were: a) to create a pool of master artisan-printers; b) to develop a group of American artists of diverse styles in the medium; c) to habituate each artist and artisan to intimate collaboration; d) to stimulate new markets; e) to guide the artisan in earning his living outside of subsidy; f) to restore the prestige of lithography by creating a collection of extraordinary prints.

3. WAYNE, D.32.

4. WAYNE, D.33.

5. TABAK, C.67, Part 1, p.29.

6. JONES-POPESCU, B.72, p.79.

7. ADAMS, B.1, p.202.

8. GOLDMAN, C.30, Part 1, pp.105–107: 'Examining the lithographs from Tamarind's Los Angeles period, it becomes clear that Tamarind's educational success was not equalled esthetically . . . The esthetic failing was an educational sacrifice. Tamarind was above all an educational conception, and teaching took priority over art.'

9. WAYNE, C.73.

10. WAYNE, C.72.

11. SMITH, C.63, p.24.

12. WAYNE, D.32.

13. ADAMS, D.1.

14. HOLLANDER, D.17.

15. SANCHEZ, D.23.

16. Clinton ADAMS points out that Tamarind (then as now) only allows the printing element to be drawn by someone other than the artist if the image is entirely geometric without personal 'handwriting'. See ADAMS, D.2.

17. ADAMS/ANTREASIAN, B.2.

18. Garo Antreasian's paper, 'Studio Paper Testing: The Tamarind Lithography Workshop 1960-1970', in LONG, ed., A.27, pp.50–52.

19. WAYNE, D.32.

20. This figure comes from Clinton Adams. The names of the Los Angeles printers are listed in *Fifty Artists Fifty Printers* (New Mexico: University of New Mexico Art Museum, 1985), 23.

21. JONES-POPESCU, B.72.

22. Irwin Hollander, master printer at Tamarind

when Ken Tyler first went there on a Foundation grant, interviewed by Pat Gilmour. See HOLLANDER, D.17.

The concept of collaboration
1. See entry for 'art' in WILLIAMS, B.121, pp.32–35.

2. Quoted in GEDEON, B.52, p.13.

3. Oxford English Dictionary.

4. The complete text of *La lithographie originale en couleurs* (1898) by André Mellerio, translated by Margaret Needham, appears in CATE, B.26, pp.79–99.

5. JONES-POPESCU says that although the Los Angeles printer Lynton Kistler believed he had invented the idea in 1946, Grant Arnold had been using a printer's chop since 1934. See B.72.

6. HAMILTON, D.16.

7. Tanya Grosman quoted in TOMKINS, C.68, p.45 – 'Barnett Newman said a wonderful thing: he said that printing is like music — the artist is the composer and the printer is the interpreter. And the interpreter is so important!'.

8. When Joe Tilson quoted Prater in an appreciation written about the printer's 1970 exhibition, he pointed out that although without a conductor music could exist in manuscript form, without Prater, none of the work in the exhibition would have been given 'the precise form and meaning that his love and dedication and technical mastery give it'. See ALLEY, B.5, n.p.

9. June Wayne, letter to Pat Gilmour, dated 9 January 1984, but actually 1985.

10. ANTREASIAN, C.4, p.185.

11. ANTREASIAN, D.10.

12. TYLER, D.25.

13. Richard S. Field, letter to Thelma Kase, 25 January 1972. Quoted in KASE, B.77.

14. FIELD, C.21, p.27.

15. RUSSELL, C.59, section C, p.24.

Tyler on the west coast: 1963–1973

Tyler's training
1. Ken Tyler interviewed by Thelma KASE, 14 February 1972. Comparing Tyler to Tanya Grosman, KASE commented that: 'Ken Tyler has a physically powerful presence which dominates his workshop, Gemini G.E.L., in a totally different way. He is vociferous, eloquent, amiable and exacting'. See B.77.

2. TYLER, D.25.

3. Ken Tyler in LONG, ed., A.27, p.50.

4. TYLER, D.25.

5. TYLER, D.26.

6. Ken Tyler quoted in KNIGIN/ZIMILES, A.21.

7. SHERRILL, A.42, p.54.

8. GOLDMAN, A.14, p.53. The article brought angry letters from Garo Antreasian and June Wayne (published in Artnews [January 1978], pp.34, 36). They criticized Goldman for her inaccuracy in calling Tyler 'research director', as the position never existed. June Wayne added: 'Tyler says "Tamarind didn't know anything about it" as though he personally invented the industrial revolution. In fact, dozens of printers and curators researched paper, inks, stone substitutes, machines and a myriad of tools and technical improvisations. The Tamarind Institute is actively conducting research and has been issuing research results on a regular basis. Tyler himself received two research grants from Tamarind, as did others, so his was hardly the Walter Mitty solo flight that the article conjures up . . . The Gemini "technological mystique" frequently used Tamarind as a straw man of old hat traditionalism until Tyler left Gemini. Now the same old canards appear in Bedford PR although Tyler presumably has discovered "the very old methods". Will he now put down Tamarind as pejoratively technological . . .?'.

9. Garo Antreasian in LONG, ed., A.27, p.50.

10. TYLER, D.29.

11. Ken Tyler, telephone conversation with Pat Gilmour, January 1985.

12. Judith Goldman, 'Twenty-Five Years of American Prints and Printmaking: 1956–1981', in STASIK, ed., C.65, p.11.

13. KNIGIN/ZIMILES, A.21.

14. Prater produced this print for the artist Gordon House (cat. no. 82) who contributes an essay, 'Spring 1959. My First Visit to Kelpra Studio', in GILMOUR and others, B.58, pp.57–58.

15. TYLER, D.26.

16. ALLEY, B.5.

17. GILMOUR and others, B.58.

18. This definition, the essential part of which reads: '. . . with the exclusion of any and all mechanical or photomechanical processes . . .', is quoted in translation in ZIGROSSER/GAEHDE, B.122, p.89.

19. ZIGROSSER/GAEHDE, B.122, p.35.

Josef Albers
1. TYLER, D.26.

2. A reviewer of Moholy-Nagy's Der Sturm exhibition said: 'Don't talk about coldness, mechanization, this is sensuality refined to its most sublimated expression'. Quoted in CAREY/GRIFFITHS, B.22, p.221.

3. TYLER, D.25.

4. ALBERS, D.3.

5. ADAMS, D.1.

6. The Saturday Review, 26 June 1965.

7. ALBERS, D.3.

8. ALBERS, D.9.

9. Print Collector's Newsletter, A.33, pp.7, 8.

10. KASE, B.77, p.107.

11. When Tyler left the partnership in 1973, the business continued under the joint direction of Felsen and Grinstein.

12. WELLIVER, C.74, p.69.

13. ALBERS, D.9.

14. TYLER, D.26.

15. ALBERS, D.6.

16. TYLER, D.26.

Robert Rauschenberg
1. SHIREY, A.43.

2. GOLDMAN, A.12, p.31.

3. DONSON, B.39, p.220.

4. LOZINGOT, D.21.

5. SOMMERS, C.64, p.25.

6. KRAMER, A.22.

7. A signature print is virtually a copy of a drawing or painting which the artist validates by signing.

8. KASE, B.77.

9. Artist's worknotes of 1962 quoted in FOSTER, B.49.

10. HUGHES, C.39, p.64.

11. CASTLEMAN, B.23, p.168.

12. FINE, A.10, p.48.

13. HUGHES, C.39, p.64.

14. Print Collector's Newsletter, A.34, p.198.

15. DAVIS, C.18, p.92.

16. YOUNG, C.81, p.25.

17. Double-page spread collage by the artist in Studio International. See C.53.

18. ALLOWAY, B.6, p.134.

19. LEVINSON, A.25, pp.26, 29.

Jasper Johns
1. FIELD, B.44, n.p.

2. YOUNG, C.76, p.53.

3. As above, p.52.

4. FINE, A.10, p.51.

5. YOUNG, C.76, p.51.

6. As above, p.52.

7. YOUNG, C.80.

8. YOUNG, A.59, p.72.

9. ADAMS, D.1.

10. TYLER, D.25.

11. YOUNG, C.76, p.52.

12. HUGHES, A.19, p.56.

13. FIELD, B.45.

14. As above, p.14.

15. As above.

16. CRICHTON, B.34, p.48.

17. FIELD, B.45, p.30.

Pop artists
1. GOLDMAN, A.12, p.30.

2. Reprint of 'What is Pop Art', Roy Lichtenstein interviewed by G. R. Svenson, in COPLANS, ed., B.32, p.52.

3. As above, p.55.

4. YOUNG, C.78, p.51.

5. 'Lichtenstein at Gemini' in COPLANS, ed., B.32, p.95.

6. Roy Lichtenstein, interviewed by Diane Waldman, in COPLANS, ed., B.32, p.109.

Claes Oldenburg and the multiple
1. Janet Daley's introduction, 'Anti-Multiples', in B.91, pp.3–4.

2. MAT = Multiplication Arts Transformable.

3. KRAMER, A.22.

4. BANHAM, C.8.

5. HULTÉN, B.69, p.12.

6. *Print Collector's Newsletter*, A.33, p.11.

7. SHERRILL, A.42, p.51.

8. GOLDMAN, C.29, p.118.

9. ROSE, C.57, p.255.

10. GOLDMAN, A.13, p.20.

11. TUCHMAN, ed., B.110, p.242.

12. For Tyler's full account of the making of the *Icebag*, see TUCHMAN, ed., B.110, pp. 254–260.

13. TUCHMAN, ed., B.110, p.265.

14. CASTLEMAN, A.3, p.25.

Frank Stella and the offset press
1. DAVIS/MURATA, B.37, p.9. One of the first exhibitions devoted to fine art in offset lithography was by R. S. FIELD and Louise SPERLING. See B.46.

2. GOLDSTON, D.15.

3. AXSOM/FLOYD/ROHN, B.12, p.16: 'In 1972 he was among the first artists to adapt offset lithography to fine art printing', and (p.97) 'Stella was one of the first printmakers to adopt this type of press for the making of fine art lithographs.'

4. June Wayne, letter to Pat Gilmour, 28 January 1985: 'I did not object to offset per se having worked with it in the *Fables* of '55. But focus is part of what one has to do . . .'

5. BRATTINGA, C.9.

6. GILMOUR, B.56, pp.97–107.

7. See GILMOUR, B.54, p.77.

8. HAYTER, B.67, pp.70, 71, and fig. 40 opp. p.99.

9. *Print Collector's Newsletter*, A.34, p.192.

10. STELLA, D.24.

11. SHIREY, A.43.

12. YOUNG, C.79, p.79.

Tyler on the east coast: 1974–1985

After the ecstasy, the laundry
1. GOLDMAN, A.14, p.54.

2. TYLER, D.26.

3. TYLER, D.25.

4. GOLDMAN, A.14, p.51.

5. ROSIN, C.58, p.63.

6. HULTÉN, B.69, p.173.

7. Ken Tyler in LONG, ed., A.27, p.92.

8. WALKER, B.114, p.19.

9. HOLLANDER, D.17.

10. Kathan Brown remembers this remark from one of S. W. Hayter's lectures. See BROWN, D.11.

11. 'Picture of a Publisher' (introduction) in GOLDMAN, B.61, n.p.

12. GOLDMAN, A.14, p.54.

13. TYLER, D.25.

14. ISENBERG, C.40, p.68.

15. DeCHILLO, A.9.

16. TYLER, D.25.

17. BROWN, D.11.

The exploration of paper
1. LONG, ed., A.27, p.79.

2. As above.

3. The story is told in Marlene Schiller, 'Machine and Moldmade Papers', in MEYER, C.47, p.45.

4. Larry Hardy in D.30.

5. Tyler's definition of 'couching' appears in SCHLOSSER/TYLER, A.40: 'Transferring the wet, newly-formed sheet of paper from the mould by pressure to a wet felt'.

6. PINDELL, C.51.

7. TYLER, D.27.

8. Rauschenberg, taking part in a symposium at Japanese International Paper Conference in Kyoto, 21 February 1983.

9. YOUNG, C.81, p.27.

10. Wilfer now works almost exclusively with the artist Chuck Close in New York City. The extent to which Tyler crops up in everybody's conversation is indicated by Close's comments in an interview with Pat Gilmour. Close said that Wilfer had joked to him that he was going to call his papermaking operation 'Tippecanoe and . . .' This was so that when Tyler went out of business Wilfer could take him on as hired help and complete his Company's name to read 'Tippecanoe and Tyler too'. The joke, somewhat obscure to non-Americans, rests on a famous nineteenth-century Presidential campaign slogan. The Presidential candidate was nicknamed Tippecanoe because of a notable victory against the Indians; his running mate for the vice-presidency was a man named Tyler. See D.12.

Paper in Bedford Village
1. FELSEN, D.13.

2. Ken Tyler in LONG, ed., A.27, p.80.

3. Noland took part in the panel discussion recorded in A.27. GOLDMAN, A.15, provides detailed drawings and photographs showing exactly how the artist's paperworks were made.

4. See GILMOUR/WILLSFORD, B.59 (the Australian National Gallery's inaugural exhibition catalogue), for text about paperwork by many different artists and extensive bibliography.

5. STANGOS, ed., B.106, p.9.

6. At the time, Tyler's maximum sheet size was 52 × 32 inches, but by the 1980s he was making sheets measuring 66 × 51 inches for Frank Stella. At the 1983 International Paper Conference in Kyoto, Japanese papermakers, using a flexible screen and overhead hoist, were able to couch a sheet 6 metres square, which was at that time said to be the largest sheet ever made.

7. Information given by David Hockney at the International Paper Conference in Kyoto, Japan, 21 February 1983.

8. STANGOS, ed., B.106, p.100.

The painter-printmakers
1. Robert Motherwell quoted in TERENZIO, B.107, p.128.

2. Ken Tyler quoted in TERENZIO, B.107, p.84.

3. WAGSTAFF, D.31.

4. Information from the dealer Brooke Alexander given in TERENZIO, B.107, pp.122, 124.

5. Ken Tyler quoted in TERENZIO, B.107, p.89.

6. Irwin Hollander quoted in TERENZIO, B.107, p.26.

7. Ken Tyler quoted in TERENZIO, B.107, p.90.

8. As above.

9. Robert Motherwell in panel discussion, 'A Special Genius . . .', quoted in TERENZIO, B.107, p.136.

10. COLSMAN-FREYBERGER, C.16, p.129.

11. Robert Motherwell quoted in TERENZIO, B.108, which deals entirely with the artist's fascination with the colour black (see p.79).

12. Robert Motherwell at the dedication of the Walker Art Center, Minneapolis, 21 September 1984.

13. KRENS, ed., B.79, pp.25, 26.

14. As above, p.42.

15. As above, p.24.

16. As above, p.24.

17. As above, p.25.

18. TYLER, D.27.

19. KRENS, ed., B.79, p.31.

20. As above, cat. no. 63.

Recent developments at Bedford Village
1. As well as beautiful spit-bite etchings, Smith also made less traditional kite-like paperworks of pulp bonded to cloth.

2. Roy Lichtenstein, 28 March 1983, quoted in FINE, A.10, p.192.

3. Tyler attended the opening of the Australian National Gallery exhibition *Ken Tyler — Printer Extraordinary* on 6 June 1985 and while in Canberra conducted a two-day workshop at the Canberra School of Art. The workshop was attended by printers and artists from all over Australia.

4. CARRINGTON, C.13.

5. GILMOUR, B.54, p.130.

6. TYLER, D.27.

7. This remark and all others by Hockney from a tape-recorded conversation between Pat Gilmour and David Hockney at Bedford Village, 22 June 1985.

8. Although not published until 1971, Rosenblum's book (B.99) had been written by early 1969.

9. ROSENBLUM, B.99, p.39.

10. GOLDMAN, B.64, p.14.

11. AXSOM/FLOYD/ROHN, B.12, p.35, note 4.

12. STELLA, D.24.

13. GOLDMAN, B.64, p.15.

14. As above.

15. A 'state' is traditionally a pull from a printing matrix taken while the work is in progress. When the finished piece arises from several overprintings, various 'states' can be made as permutations and can be altered, or added to.

16. STELLA, D.24.

17. LEMON, D.19.

18. ADAMS, D.1.

19. STELLA, D.24.

20. As above.

21. As above.

22. TYLER, D.26.

23. TYLER, D.25.

24. STELLA, D.24.

25. GOLDMAN, B.64, p.14.

26. An intaglio plate is printed under such pressure that it makes three-dimensional ridges in the paper. Because of this, several different plates can, if overprinted, cause a very complex disturbance of the paper's surface.

27. ACKLEY, C.1, p.207.

28. STELLA, D.24.

29. TYLER, D.25.

30. ACKLEY, C.1, p.207.

31. WALKER, B.114, p.27.

32. See Robert Hughes, *Frank Stella* — The Swan Engravings (Fort Worth, Texas: Fort Worth Art Museum, 1984).

33. Frank Stella quoted in GOLDMAN, B.64, pp.16, 17.

34. TYLER, D.25 and D.26

Tyler's achievement

1. TYLER, D.25.

2. Frank Stella quoted in GOLDMAN, B.64, p.17.

3. STELLA, D.24.

4. TYLER, D.25.

5. As above.

6. As above.

7. As above.

8. As above.

9. *Print Collector's Newsletter*, A.34, p.196.

10. TYLER, D.25.

11. GOLDMAN, B.64, p.17.

12. TYLER, D.25.

13. As above.

14. ANTREASIAN, D.10.

15. TYLER, D.25.

16. As above.

17. TYLER, D.26.

BIBLIOGRAPHY

Note to the Bibliography

Part A of this bibliography lists those publications which deal almost exclusively with Tyler or the firms he founded, including the promotional brochures published by Gemini G.E.L. during the period in which he was Director. List A reveals that during 1970/71 Tyler was featured not only in the specialist press, but also in mass circulation magazines such as *Life* and *Time*. The list of publications about Tyler will be expanded in 1986 by two volumes to be published by the Walker Art Center, where the Tyler Graphics study archive is housed. Throughout his career, Tyler's most faithful chronicler has been Judith Goldman, but Joseph E. Young, strategically placed on the west coast of America during Tyler's formative period, has contributed a number of key interviews with artists which throw important light on the printer's contribution.

While in the past the organizing principle for exhibitions of artists' prints has been characterized almost exclusively by individual artists or artists' groups and very occasionally by publishers, in the past two decades there has been a marked tendency for exhibitions to centre on the role of the printer, or the publisher who undertakes printing in-house. (See A.1, A.3, A.10, A.11, B.4, B.5, B.11, B.14, B.15, B.17, B.25, B.31, B.38, B.40, B.50, B.52, B.55, B.56, B.58, B.80, B.82, B.88, B.102, B.104, B.107, B.116, B.117.) Significantly, the print collection of the Tate Gallery in London, formed as recently as 1974–75, was drawn mainly from the archival prints retained by printers working closely with artists. An important addition to the above list, due for publication in 1987, is Esther Sparks' book provisionally entitled *Universal Limited Art Editions — A History and Catalogue Raisonné*, with an introduction by Amei Wallach. The publications recognizing the importance of the printer cannot be exhaustively listed here, but in recent years an increasing flow of periodical articles has dealt with the printer's contribution. In America the subject has been given special attention by Clinton Adams and Janet Flint, whose articles are listed in the bibliography of Adams' definitive book, *American Lithographers 1900–1960*, interestingly subtitled *The Artists and their Printers*. The importance of this development is also attested to by the incidence of significant references to Tyler in books which span the entire history of twentieth century printmaking (see B.23, B.54, B.71, B.115).

Bibliography

Contents

A.   Books, catalogues and articles in periodicals by or about Tyler, or about the firms he has founded
B.   Books and catalogues of general interest [*indicates significant mention of Tyler or the firms he has founded]
C.   Articles of general interest in periodicals [*indicates significant mention of Tyler or the firms he has founded]
D.   Unpublished sources — interviews, letters and manuscripts

NOTE: The citations in each of the four sections of this bibliography are numbered within each section. The citations are listed alphabetically by author, or title (when no author or editor is known) and then chronologically for each author.

Dates that appear in parentheses indicate that the year of publication has been determined from external evidence.

Part A

Books, catalogues, and articles in periodicals by or about Tyler, or about the firms he has founded

A.1   ARMSTRONG, Elizabeth.
Prints from Tyler Graphics.
Minneapolis: Walker Art Center, 1984.

A.2   BRACH, P.
Lithographs From Gemini.
San Diego: San Diego Art Gallery, University of California, 1968.

A.3   CASTLEMAN, Riva.
Technics and Creativity: Gemini G.E.L.
New York: Museum of Modern Art, 1971.

A.4   *Claes Oldenburg: Geometric Mouse – Scale C.*
Los Angeles: Gemini G.E.L., 1971.

A.5   COPLANS, John.
Frank Stella: The V Series.
Los Angeles: Gemini G.E.L., 1968.

A.6   COPLANS, John.
Ellsworth Kelly.
Los Angeles: Gemini G.E.L., 1970.

A.7   COPLANS, John.
Roy Lichtenstein: Graphics, Reliefs & Sculpture 1969–1970.
Los Angeles: Gemini G.E.L., 1970.

A.8   CRUTCHFIELD, William.
Americana.
Los Angeles: Gemini G.E.L., 1967.

A.9   DeCHILLO, Suzanne.
'Meeting Ground for Art and Print'.
New York Times, 11 March 1979, 17.

A.10 FINE, Ruth E.
Gemini G.E.L., Art and Collaboration.
New York: Abbeville Press in association with the National Gallery of Art, Washington, D.C., 1984.

A.11 GILMOUR, Pat.
Ken Tyler – Master Printer, and the American Printmaking Renaissance. Canberra: Australian National Gallery in association with Hudson Hills Press, New York, 1986. (Abridged version with checklist to the exhibition *Ken Tyler: Printer Extraordinary*, Australian National Gallery, 1985.)

A.12 GOLDMAN, Judith.
'Gemini Prints at the Museum of Modern Art'. *Print Collector's Newsletter* (May–June 1971): 30, 31.

A.13 GOLDMAN, Judith.
Art off the Picture Press: Tyler Graphics Ltd. Hempstead, New York: Emily Lowe Gallery, Hofstra University, 1977.

A.14 GOLDMAN, Judith.
'The Master Printer of Bedford, N.Y.' *Artnews* (September 1977): 50–54.

A.15 GOLDMAN, Judith.
Kenneth Noland: Handmade Papers. Bedford Village, New York: Tyler Graphics, 1978.

A.16 HARVEY, Donald.
Seven Artists at Tyler Graphics Ltd. Ohio: Trisolini Gallery, Ohio University College of Fine Arts, 1979.

A.17 'A Heart of Stone'.
Western Printer & Lithographer (April 1968): 16–17.

A.18 HOPPS, Walter.
Jasper Johns: Fragments – According to What. Los Angeles: Gemini G.E.L., 1971.

A.19 HUGHES, Robert.
'Gemini Rising: The Print Renaissance'. *Time*, 18 January 1971, 56–57.

A.20 *Ken Price: Interior Series.* Los Angeles: Gemini G.E.L., 1971.

A.21 KNIGIN, M., and ZIMILES, M.
Statement by Kenneth Tyler in *The Contemporary Lithography Workshop around the World.* New York: Van Nostrand Reinholt, 1974.

A.22 KRAMER, Hilton.
'Technics of Fashion'. *New York Times*, 2 May 1971, Section 2, p.21.

A.23 LARSEN, Susan.
'Putting Inspiration on Press'. *Mainliner* (February 1980): 90–96.

A.24 LEIDER, Philip.
Frank Stella: Star of Persia I & II, Black Series I. Los Angeles: Gemini G.E.L., 1967.

A.25 LEVINSON, Robert S.
'Gemini and the Rebirth of Graphics'. *Los Angeles Times*, 24 January 1971, 24–29.

A.26 LIPPARD, Lucy.
Robert Rauschenberg: Booster and 7 Studies.

A.27 LONG, Paulette, ed.
Paper — Art & Technology: Based on Presentations given at the International Paper Conference held in San Francisco, March 1978. San Francisco: World Print Council, 1979.

Los Angeles: Gemini G.E.L., 1967.

A.28 *Man Ray.* Los Angeles: Gemini G.E.L., 1967.

A.29 NODELMAN, Sheldon, and TYLER, Kenneth E.
Josef Albers: Embossed Linear Constructions. Los Angeles: Gemini G.E.L., 1969.

A.30 NORDLAND, Gerald, and TYLER, Kenneth E.
Josef Albers: White Embossings on Gray. Los Angeles: Gemini G.E.L., 1971.

A.31 OLDENBURG, Claes.
A History of The Double-Nose/Purse/ Punching Bag/Ashtray Multiple. Los Angeles: Gemini G.E.L., 1970.

A.32 'Original Art, Hot Off the Presses'.
Life (23 January 1970): 57–61.

A.33 'Pricing Prints or the Poorman's Art?'.
[Panel discussion between Kenneth Tyler, René Block, Sylvan Cole, Marian Goodman, John Loring and Jo Miller, 25 November 1974.] *Print Collector's Newsletter* (March 1975): 4–11.

A.34 'Printing Today: Eight Views'.
[Panel discussion between Kenneth Tyler, Pat Branstead, Chip Elwell, Alexander Heinrici, Jack Lemon, Bud Shark, Judith Solodkin and Jeff Wasserman, 30 October 1982.] *Print Collector's Newsletter* (January– February 1983): 189–200.

A.35 *Richard Serra.* Los Angeles: Gemini G.E.L., 1972.

A.36 *Robert Rauschenberg:* Cardbirds. Los Angeles: Gemini G.E.L., 1971.

A.37 *Robert Rauschenberg:* Pages *and* Fuses. Los Angeles: Gemini G.E.L., 1974.

A.38 ROSE, Barbara.
Claes Oldenburg: Notes. Los Angeles: Gemini G.E.L., 1968.

A.39 ROSE, Barbara.
Figurine Cups by Ken Price. Los Angeles: Gemini G.E.L., 1970.

A.40 SCHLOSSER, Leonard, and TYLER, Kenneth E.
Paper and Printmaking Glossary. Privately published, 1978.

A.41 SCHNEIDER, Pierre.
Sam Francis at Gemini. Los Angeles: Gemini G.E.L., 1971.

A.42 SHERRILL, Robert.
'Gemini G.E.L.: Interview with Kenneth Tyler'.

Lithopinion (Summer 1970): 51–61.

A.43 SHIREY, David L.
'Modern Museum Offers Works of
"Multiple" Art'.
New York Times, 6 May 1971, 52.

A.44 SOLOMON, Alan.
Jasper Johns: Lead Reliefs.
Los Angeles: Gemini G.E.L., 1969.

A.45 TUTEN, Frederic.
Lithographs from Gemini.
Davis, California: Memorial Union Art Gallery,
University of California, 1969.

A.46 TYLER, Kenneth E.
Josef Albers: Embossed Linear
Constructions.
Los Angeles: Gemini G.E.L., 1969.

A.47 TYLER, Kenneth E.
Robert Motherwell: Summer Light Series.
Los Angeles: Gemini G.E.L., 1973.

A.48 TYLER, Kenneth E.
*Ed Baynard: Woodblock Prints and
Watercolored Lithographs.*
Bedford Village, New York: Tyler Graphics
(1980).

A.49 TYLER, Kenneth E.
Richard Smith: Cartouche Series.
Saskatchewan, Canada: Mackenzie Art
Gallery, University of Regina, 1981.

A.50 TYLER, Kenneth E.
'Experiences with Paper'.
In A.27, pp.78–80.

A.51 TYLER, Kenneth E., and FELSEN,
Rosamund.
'Two Rauschenberg Paper Projects'.
In A.27, pp.81–83.

A.52 TYLER, Kenneth E.
'Experimental Approaches to Paper in Art'.
[Panel discussion with Riva Castleman,
Robert Flynn Johnson, Kenneth Noland and
Garner Tullis.]
In A.27, pp.87–96.

A.53 TYLER, Kenneth E.
'Supporting an Apprenticeship Program'.
[Lecture given at Purchase, April 1978.]
Washington D.C.: National Endowment for
the Arts, 1981.

A.54 TYLER, Kenneth E.; ALBERS, Josef; and
HOPKINS, Henry T.
Josef Albers: White Line Squares.
Los Angeles: Los Angeles County Museum
of Art and Gemini G.E.L., 1966.

A.55 VON MEIER, K.
Lithographs, Gemini G.E.L.
San Antonio, Texas: San Antonio Art League
and Museum Association, 1968.

A.56 WHITNEY, David.
Robert Rauschenberg: Reels (B + C).
Los Angeles: Gemini G.E.L., 1968.

A.57 *Willem de Kooning:* Untitled.
Los Angeles: Gemini G.E.L., 1972.

A.58 YOUNG, Joseph E.

Recent Prints from Gemini.
Los Angeles: Los Angeles County Museum
of Art, 1970.

A.59 YOUNG, Joseph E.
'Los Angeles Gemini G.E.L.'
Art International (20 December 1971): 7.

Part B

Books and catalogues of general interest
[*indicates significant mention of Tyler or the firms
he has founded]

B.1 ADAMS, Clinton.
*American Lithographers, 1900–1960: The
Artists and Their Printers.*
Albuquerque, New Mexico: University of
New Mexico Press, 1983.

B.2 *ADAMS, Clinton, and ANTREASIAN,
Garo Z.
*The Tamarind Book of Lithography: Art &
Techniques.*
Los Angeles: Tamarind Lithography
Workshop in association with Abrams,
1971.

B.3 ALBERS, Josef.
Interaction of Color.
New Haven, Connecticut: Yale University
Press, 1963. Rev. ed. 1975.

B.4 ALLEN, Virginia.
Tamarind: Homage to Lithography.
New York: Museum of Modern Art, 1969;
New Plymouth, New Zealand: Govett-
Brewster Art Gallery, 1973.

B.5 ALLEY, Ronald.
Kelpra Prints.
London: Arts Council of Great Britain,
1970.

B.6 ALLOWAY, Lawrence.
Topics in American Art.
New York: W. W. Norton, 1975.

B.7 ALLOWAY, Lawrence.
Robert Rauschenberg.
Washington, D.C.: National Collection of
Fine Arts, 1976.

B.8 ALLOWAY, Lawrence.
Roy Lichtenstein.
New York: Abbeville Press, 1983.

B.9 ARMSTRONG, Thomas, and CRICHTON,
Michael.
Jasper Johns.
London: Thames and Hudson, 1977.

B.10 ARNASON, H. H.
Robert Motherwell.
New York: Abrams, 1982.

B.11 *L'Arte della Stampa.*
Rome: Galleria Nazionale d'Arte Moderna,
1974.

B.12 *AXSOM, Richard H; FLOYD, Phylis; and
ROHN, Matthew.
*The Prints of Frank Stella: A Catalogue
Raisonnè 1967–1982.*

New York: Hudson Hills Press in association with University of Michigan Museum of Art, Ann Arbor, 1983.

B.13 BAKER, E. C.
Ellsworth Kelly: Recent Paintings and Sculpture.
New York: Metropolitan Museum of Art, 1979.

B.14 BARO, Gene, and SAFF, Donald.
Graphicstudio, U.S.F.: An Experiment in Art and Education.
Brooklyn, New York: Brooklyn Museum, 1978.

B.15 *BEAL, Graham W. J.
Artist and Printer: Six American Print Studios.
Minneapolis: Walker Art Center, 1980.

B.16 BIANCHINI, Paul.
Roy Lichtenstein: Drawings and Prints.
New York: Chelsea House Publishers, 1970.

B.17 BLOCH, Maurice E.
Words and Images — Universal Limited Art Editions.
Los Angeles: Wright Art Gallery, University of California, 1978.

B.18 BOGLE, A.
Graphic Works by Edward Ruscha.
Auckland, New Zealand: Auckland City Art Gallery, 1978.

B.19 BRIGHTON, Andrew.
David Hockney: Prints 1954–1977.
Nottingham, England: Midland Group Gallery in association with Petersburg Press, 1979.

B.20 BRUGGEN, Coosje van.
Claes Oldenburg: Drawings, Watercolors and Prints.
Stockholm: Moderna Museet, 1970.

B.21 BUCHER, François.
Josef Albers: Despite Straight Lines: An Analysis of his Graphic Constructions.
Cambridge, Massachusetts: MIT Press, 1977.

B.22 CAREY, Frances, and GRIFFITHS, Antony.
The Print in Germany 1880–1933.
London: British Museum, 1984.

B.23 *CASTLEMAN, Riva.
Prints of the Twentieth Century: A History.
London: Thames and Hudson, 1976.

B.24 CASTLEMAN, Riva.
Printed Art: A View of Two Decades.
New York: Museum of Modern Art, 1980.

B.25 CATE, Phillip Dennis.
The Rutgers Archives for Printmaking Studios.
New Brunswick, New Jersey: Zimmerli Art Museum, Rutgers University, 1983.

B.26 CATE, Phillip Dennis, and HITCHINGS, Sinclair H.
The Color Revolution: Color Lithography in France 1890–1900.

New Brunswick, New Jersey: Rutgers University Art Gallery, 1978.

B.27 *Claes Oldenburg.*
London: Arts Council of Great Britain, 1970.

B.28 *Claes Oldenburg: Drawings and Prints.*
New York: Chelsea House Publishers, 1969.

B.29 *Claes Oldenburg: Six Themes.*
Minneapolis: Walker Art Center, 1975.

B.30 COHEN, Arthur.
Robert Motherwell: Selected Prints 1961–1974.
New York: Brooke Alexander, 1974.

B.31 CONTENSOU, Bernadette.
L'Atelier Lacourière-Frelaut ou 50 Ans de Gravure et d'Imprimerie en Taille-Douce 1929–1979.
Paris: Musée d'Art Moderne de la Ville de Paris, 1979.

B.32 *COPLANS, John, ed.
Roy Lichtenstein.
London: Allen Lane, The Penguin Press, 1973.

B.33 COWART, Jack.
Roy Lichtenstein, 1970–1980.
New York: Hudson Hills Press in association with the St. Louis Art Museum, 1981.

B.34 *CRICHTON, Michael.
Jasper Johns.
New York: Whitney Museum of American Art in association with Abrams (1978).

B.35 *David Hockney: Paintings, Prints and Drawings 1960–1970.*
London: Whitechapel Art Gallery, 1970.

B.36 *David Hockney: Prints and Drawings.*
New Haven, Connecticut: Yale Center for British Art, 1978.

B.37 DAVIS, Hanlyn, and MURATA, Hiroshi.
Art and Technology — Offset Prints.
Bethlehem, Pennsylvania: Lehigh University, 1983.

B.38 DEAN, Sonia.
The Artist and the Printer: Lithographs 1966–1981, a Collection of Printer's Proofs.
Melbourne: National Gallery of Victoria, 1982.

B.39 *DONSON, Theodore B.
Prints and the Print Market.
New York: Thomas Y. Crowell, 1977.

B.40 *Ediciones Poligrafa, Barcelona.*
London: Redfern Gallery, 1979.

B.41 *Edward Kienholz.*
Los Angeles: Los Angeles County Museum of Art, 1966.

B.42 *Edward Kienholz: Works from the 1960s.*
Washington, D.C.: Washington Gallery of Modern Art, 1967.

B.43   Feinblatt, Ebria, and DAVIS, Bruce.
Los Angeles Prints, 1883–1980.
Los Angeles: Los Angeles County Museum
of Art, 1980.

B.44   *FIELD, Richard S.
Jasper Johns: Prints 1960–1970.
Philadelphia: Philadelphia Museum of Art in
association with Praeger, 1970.

B.45   *FIELD, Richard S.
Jasper Johns: Prints 1970–1977.
London: Petersburg Press in association
with Wesleyan University Press, 1978.

B.46   FIELD, Richard S., and SPERLING, Louise.
Offset Lithography.
Middletown, Connecticut: Wesleyan
University Press, 1973.

B.47   FLINT, Janet.
*The Prints of Louis Lozowick:
A Catalogue Raisonné.*
New York: Hudson Hills Press, 1982.

B.48   FORGE, Andrew.
Rauschenberg.
New York: Abrams, 1969.

B.49   *FOSTER, Edward A.
*Robert Rauschenberg: Prints,
1948–1970.*
Minneapolis: Minneapolis Institute of Arts,
1970.

B.50   FRANCIS, Sam, and PAGE, George.
*Sam Francis: The Litho Shop,
1970–1979.*
New York: Brooke Alexander, 1979.

B.51   FRIEDMAN, Martin.
Oldenburg: Six Themes.
Minneapolis: Walker Art Center, 1975.

B.52   GEDEON, Lucinda H.
*Tamarind: From Los Angeles to
Albuquerque.*
Los Angeles: Grunwald Center for the
Graphic Arts, University of California,
1985.

B.53   GEELHAAR, Christian.
Jasper Johns: Working Proofs.
London: Petersburg Press, 1980.

B.54   *GILMOUR, Pat.
Modern Prints.
London and New York: Studio Vista, 1970.

B.55   GILMOUR, Pat.
*Lithographs from the Curwen Studio:
A Retrospective of Fifteen Years
Printmaking.*
London: Camden Arts Centre, 1973.

B.56   GILMOUR, Pat.
Artists at Curwen.
London: Tate Gallery, 1977.

B.57   GILMOUR, Pat.
*Understanding Prints: A Contemporary
Guide.*
London: Waddington Galleries, 1979.

B.58   GILMOUR, Pat, and others.
Kelpra Studio.
London: Tate Gallery, 1980.

B.59   *GILMOUR, Pat, and WILLSFORD, Anne.
Paperwork.
Canberra: Australian National Gallery,
1982.

B.60   GLAZEBROOK, Mark.
*David Hockney: Paintings, Prints and
Drawings, 1960–1970.*
London: Whitechapel Art Gallery, 1970.

B.61   GOLDMAN, Judith.
*Brooke Alexander: A Decade of Print
Publishing.*
Boston: Boston University Art Gallery (*c.*
1978).

B.62   *GOLDMAN, Judith.
American Prints: Process & Proofs.
New York: Whitney Museum of American
Art, 1981.

B.63   GOLDMAN, Judith.
Jasper Johns: Prints 1977–1981.
Boston: Segal Gallery, 1981.

B.64   *GOLDMAN, Judith.
*Frank Stella: Fourteen Prints with
Drawings, Collages and Working Proofs.*
Princeton, New Jersey: Princeton
University Art Museum, 1983.

B.65   GOLDMAN, Judith.
Frank Stella: Prints 1967–1982.
New York: Whitney Museum of American
Art, 1983.

B.66   *HAMILTON, Richard.
Collected Words 1953–1982.
London: Thames and Hudson, 1982.

B.67   HAYTER, S. W.
About Prints.
London: Oxford University Press, 1962.

B.68   HOCKNEY, David.
David Hockney by David Hockney.
Ed. N. Stangos.
London: Thames and Hudson, 1975.

B.69   HULTÉN, K. G. P.
*The Machine as Seen at the End of the
Mechanical Age.*
New York: Museum of Modern Art in
association with New York Graphic
Society, 1968.

B.70   JANSON, H. W., and JANSON, Dora Jane.
A History of Art.
London: Thames and Hudson, 1962.

B.71   *JOHNSON, Una E.
American Prints and Printmakers.
Garden City, New York: Doubleday, 1980.

B.72   JONES-POPESCU, Elizabeth.
'American Lithography and Tamarind
Lithography Workshop/Tamarind Institute
1900–1980'.
Ph.D. diss., University of New Mexico,
1980.

B.73   *Josef Albers at the Metropolitan Museum
of Art: An Exhibition of his Paintings and
Prints.*

New York: Metropolitan Museum of Art, 1971.

B.74   *Josef Albers: Paintings and Graphics, 1917–1970.*
Princeton, New Jersey: Princeton University Art Museum, 1971.

B.75   * *Josef Albers:* White Line Squares.
Los Angeles: Los Angeles County Museum of Art in association with Gemini G.E.L., 1966.

B.76   KAINEN, Jacob.
Photography in Printmaking.
Washington, D.C.: National Collection of Fine Arts, 1968.

B.77   *KASE, Thelma Green.
'The Artist, the Printer and the Publisher: A Study in Printing Partnerships 1960-1970'.
M.A. thesis, University of Missouri, 1973.

B.78   KOZLOFF, Max.
Jasper Johns.
New York: Abrams, 1967.

B.79   *KRENS, Thomas, ed.
Helen Frankenthaler Prints: 1961–1979.
New York: Harper & Row in association with Williams College, 1980.

B.80   *Landfall Press: A Survey of Contemporary Prints (1970–1977).*
Chicago: Museum of Contemporary Art, 1977.

B.81   LANE, John R., and LARSEN, Susan C., eds.
Abstract Paintings and Sculpture in America 1927–44.
New York: Museum of Art, Carnegie Institute in association with Abrams, 1983.

B.82   *LARSON, P.
Prints from Gemini G.E.L.: Johns, Kelly, Lichtenstein, Motherwell, Nauman, Rauschenberg, Serra, Stella.
Minneapolis: Walker Art Center, 1974.

B.83   LEGG, Alicia.
Claes Oldenburg.
London: Tate Gallery in association with Museum of Modern Art, New York, 1970.

B.84   LEIDER, Philip.
Stella Singe 1970.
Fort Worth, Texas: Fort Worth Art Museum, 1978.

B.85   LIVINGSTONE, Marco.
David Hockney.
London: Thames and Hudson, 1981.

B.86   LIVINSTON, Jane, and TUCKER, Marcia.
Bruce Nauman: Work from 1965 to 1972.
Los Angeles: Los Angeles County Museum of Art, 1972.

B.87   McKENDRY, John.
Robert Motherwell's A La Pintura: *The Genesis of a Book.*
New York: Metropolitan Museum of Art, 1972.

B.88   *Master Prints from Landfall Press.*
Chicago: Smart Gallery, University of Chicago, 1980.

B.89   MILLER, Jo.
Josef Albers: Prints, 1915–1970.
Brooklyn, New York: Brooklyn Museum, 1973.

B.90   MOURLOT, Fernand.
Picasso Lithographes.
Paris: André Sauret, 1970.

B.91   *New Multiple Art.*
London: Whitechapel Art Gallery, 1970.

B.92   NORDLAND, Gerald.
Josef Albers: The American Years.
Washington, D.C.: Washington Gallery of Modern Art, 1965.

B.93   *Richard Hamilton Prints: A Complete Catalogue of Graphic Works 1939–83.*
Stuttgart and London: Edition Hansjorg Mayer, 1984.

B.94   RICHARDSON, Brenda.
Frank Stella: The Black Paintings.
Baltimore: Baltimore Museum of Art, 1977.

B.95   *Robert Motherwell: Selected Prints: 1961–1974.*
New York: Brooke Alexander, 1974.

B.96   RODMAN, Selden.
Conversations with Artists.
New York: Capricorn Books, 1961.

B.97   ROSE, Barbara, and KELLY, Ellsworth.
Ellsworth Kelly: Paintings and Sculptures, 1963–1979.
Amsterdam: Stedelijk Museum, 1980.

B.98   ROSE, Bernice.
Jackson Pollock: Drawing Into Painting.
New York: Museum of Modern Art in association with Harper & Row, 1980.

B.99   ROSENBLUM, Robert.
Frank Stella.
Harmondsworth, England: Penguin, 1971.

B.100   *Roy Lichtenstein.*
London: Tate Gallery, 1968.

B.101   RUBIN, William S.
Frank Stella.
New York: Museum of Modern Art, 1970.

B.102   SAFT, Carol.
Artist and Printer: Printmaking as a Collaborative Process.
New York: Pratt Graphics Center, 1981.

B.103   *Sam Francis: Works on Paper, a Survey 1948–1979.*
Boston: Institute of Contemporary Art, 1979.

B.104   SHAPIRA, Nathan H.
Big Prints from Rome: 2RC.
Los Angeles: Center for Contemporary Culture, 1980.

B.105   SPIES, Werner.
Josef Albers.
London: Thames and Hudson, 1971.

B.106 *STANGOS, Nikos, ed.
David Hockney: Paper Pools.
London: Thames and Hudson, 1980.

B.107 *TERENZIO, Stephanie.
The Prints of Robert Motherwell
[Catalogue Raisonné 1943-1984 by
Dorothy C. Belknap.]
New York: Hudson Hills Press in
association with the American Federation
of Arts, 1984.

B.108 TERENZIO, Stephanie.
Robert Motherwell and Black.
Storrs, Connecticut: Benton Museum,
University of Connecticut, 1980.

B.109 TOMKINS, Calvin.
*Off the Wall: Robert Rauschenberg and the
Art World of Our Time.*
New York: Doubleday, 1980.

B.110 *TUCHMAN, Maurice, ed.
*A Report on The Art and Technology
Program . . . 1967–1971.*
Los Angeles: Los Angeles County Museum
of Art, 1971.

B.111 TWYMAN, Michael.
Printing 1770–1970.
London: Eyre and Spottiswood, 1970.

B.112 WALDMAN, Diane.
Roy Lichtenstein.
New York: Solomon R. Guggenheim
Museum, 1969.

B.113 WALDMAN, Diane.
Ellsworth Kelly: Drawings, Collages, Prints.
Greenwich, Connecticut: New York
Graphic Society, 1970.

B.114 *WALKER, Barry.
The American Artist as Printmaker.
Brooklyn, New York: Brooklyn Museum,
1983.

B.115 *WATROUS, James.
*A Century of American Printmaking,
1880–1980.*
Madison, Wisconsin: University of
Wisconsin Press, 1984.

B.116 WAYNE, June.
About Tamarind.
Los Angeles: Tamarind Lithography
Workshop, 1969.

B.117 WEIDEMANN, K.
*30 Jahre Domberger, 20 Jahre Haas, 15
Jahre Kicherer: 3 Werkstätten zeigen
Serigraphien von 120 Kunstlern.*
Tübingen, Germany: Kunsthalle, 1979.

B.118 WEIERMAIT, P.
*David Hockney: Drawings and Prints,
1959–1977.*
Vienna: Albertina, 1978.

B.119 WILLETT, John.
The New Sobriety 1917–1923.
London: Thames and Hudson, 1978.

B.120 *William Crutchfield: Watercolors, Prints and
Drawings.*

New York: Dorsky Galleries, 1972.

B.121 WILLIAMS, Raymond.
Keywords.
London: Fontana, 1976.

B.122 ZIGROSSER, Carl, and GAEHDE,
Christa M.
*A Guide to the Collecting and Care of
Original Prints.*
London: Arco, 1966.

Part C

Articles of general interest in periodicals [*indicates
significant mention of Tyler or the firms he has
founded]

C.1 *ACKLEY, Clifford.
'Frank Stella's Big Football Weekend'.
Print Collector's Newsletter (January 1983):
207-208.

C.2 ALLOWAY, Lawrence.
'Rauschenberg's Graphics'.
Art and Artists (September 1970): 18-21.

C.3 ANDERSON, A.
'Scrapbooks, Notebooks, Letters, Diaries:
Artists' Books Come of Age'.
Artnews (March 1978): 68-74.

C.4 *ANTREASIAN, Garo Z.
'Some Thoughts About Printmaking and Print
Collaborations'.
Art Journal (Summer 1980): 180-188.

C.5 ASHBERY, John.
'Willem de Kooning: A Suite of New
Lithographs'.
Artnews Annual (1971): 117-138.

C.6 ATKINS, Robert.
'Frank Stella — Painter and Printmaker'.
Printnews (May–June 1983): 4-7.

C.7 AUSTIN, Gabriel.
'Alice in Dali-Land'.
Print Collector's Newsletter (May–June
1972): 25-26.

C.8 BANHAM, Reyner.
'Aesthetics of the Yellow Pages'.
New Society (1966): 271.

C.9 BRATTINGA, Pieter.
'Eugene Feldman's Creative Experiments in
Photo-Offset Lithography'.
Artist's Proof (1962): 25.

C.10 BROWN, Kathan.
'Wasting and Wasting Not: How (and Why)
Artists Work at Crown Point Press'.
Art Journal (Spring 1980): 176-179.

C.11 *BUTTERFIELD, Jan.
'David Hockney: Blue Hedonistic Pools'.
Print Collector's Newsletter (July–August
1979): 74-76.

C.12 CAFETZ, S.
'Four Early Lichtenstein Prints'.
Artist's Proof 10 (1970): 18-52.

C.13 CARRINGTON, Noel.

'Autolithography of Plastic Plates'.
Penrose Annual (1950): 64–66.

C.14 CASTLEMAN, Riva.
'Tatyana Grosman 1904–1982'.
Print Collector's Newsletter (September–October 1982): 117.

C.15 CATOIR, B.
'Interview with Edward Kienholz'.
Kunstwerk (March 1973): 49–50.

C.16 *COLSMAN-FREYBERGER, Heidi.
'Robert Motherwell: Words & Images'.
Print Collector's Newsletter
(January–February 1974): 125–129.

C.17 *COPLANS, John.
'Fragments According to Johns, an Interview with Jasper Johns'.
Print Collector's Newsletter (May–June 1972): 29–32.

C.18 *DAVIS, Douglas M.
'Rauschenberg's Recent Graphics'.
Art in America (July–August 1969): 90–95.

C.19 DAVIS, Douglas M.
'Artist of Everything' [Rauschenberg].
Newsweek, 25 October 1976, 94–99.

C.20 DIAMONSTEIN, Barbarelle.
'Inside New York's Art World: An Interview with Robert Motherwell'.
Partisan Review (1979): 376–379.

C.21 *FIELD, Richard S.
'On Originality'.
Print Collector's Newsletter (May–June 1972): 26–28.

C.22 FIELD, Richard S.
'Jasper Johns' Flags'.
Print Collector's Newsletter (July–August 1976): 69–77.

C.23 FRIED, Michael.
'Ronald Davis: Surface and Illusion'.
Artforum 5 (April 1967): 37–41.

C.24 GELDZAHLER, Henry.
'David Hockney: An Intimate View'.
Print Review (1980): 36–50.

C.25 GILMOUR, Pat.
'Symbiotic Exploitation or Collaboration: Dine & Hamilton with Crommelynck'.
Print Collector's Newsletter
(January–February 1985): 193–198.

C.26 GLASS, Laurie.
'June Wayne Graphics, Paintings and Tapestries'.
Artweek (22 May 1976).

C.27 GOLDMAN, Judith.
'Frank Stella: *Black Series* and *Star of Persia* Prints'.
Artist's Proof (1968): 67–79.

C.28 GOLDMAN, Judith.
'Print Criteria.
Artnews (January 1972): 48–51, 65.

C.29 *GOLDMAN, Judith.
'Sort of a Commercial for Objects'.

Print Collector's Newsletter
(January–February 1972): 117–121.

C.30 *GOLDMAN, Judith.
'The Print Establishment' (Parts 1 and 2).
Art in America (July–August 1973):
105–109; (September–October 1973):
102–104.

C.31 GOLDMAN, Judith.
'Printmaking: The Medium isn't the Message Anymore'.
Artnews (March 1980): 82–85.

C.32 GOLDSTEIN, C.
'Teaching Modernism: What Albers Learned in the Bauhaus and Taught to Rauschenberg, Noland and Hesse'.
Arts Magazine (December 1979): 108–116.

C.33 GOODMAN, Calvin J.
'Master Printers and Print Workshops'.
American Artist (October 1976): 67–73.

C.34 GRAFTON, Samuel.
'Tamarind: Where Artist and Craftsman Meet'.
Lithopinion, Tamarind Lithography Workshop (undated).

C.35 GRAY, Cleve.
'Tatyana Grosman's Workshop'.
Art in America (December–January 1965–66): 83–85.

C.36 HAMILTON, Richard.
'Roy Lichtenstein'.
Studio (January 1968): 20–31.

C.37 HESS, Thomas B.
'Prints: Where History, Style and Money Meet'.
Artnews (January 1972): 29, 66–67.

C.38 HUGHES, Robert.
'Enfant Terrible at 50' [Rauschenberg].
Time, 27 January 1975, 44.

C.39 HUGHES, Robert.
'The Most Living Artist' [Rauschenberg].
Time, 29 November 1976, 58, 61–64.

C.40 ISENBERG, Barbara.
'Litho Revival: Proof of the Art'.
Calendar: Los Angeles Times
(1 January 1978): 1, 68, 69.

C.41 JONES, Elizabeth.
'Robert Blackburn: An Investment in an Idea'.
The Tamarind Papers (Winter 1982–83):
10–14.

C.42 KOZLOFF, Max.
'An Interview with Robert Motherwell'.
Artforum (September 1965): 33–37.

C.43 LANGSNER, Jules.
'Is There an American Print Revival?
Tamarind Workshop'.
Artnews (January 1962): 34, 35, 58.

C.44 LEVINSON, Robert S.
'Renaissance of Lithography'.
Westways (November 1970): 6–11, 52.

C.45 *'Lithographs and Original Prints:

Lichtenstein's Graphic Works; Roy Lichtenstein in Conversation with John Coplans'.
Studio (December 1970): 264–265.

C.46   'Lithography at Tamarind'.
Time, 10 April 1964.

C.47 * MEYER, Susan E., and others.
'The Revolution in Paper'.
American Artist (August 1977): 33–49.

C.48   MICHELSON, Annette.
'The Imaginary Object: Recent Prints by Jasper Johns'.
Artist's Proof (1968): 44–49.

C.49 * 'Original Art, Hot Off the Presses'.
Life (23 January 1970): 57–61.

C.50   PHILLIPS, Deborah C.
'Artist and Printer: "A Coincidence of Sympathies" '.
Artnews (March 1981): 100–106.

C.51   PINDELL, Howardina.
'Tales of Brave Ulysses: Alan Shields Interviewed'.
Print Collector's Newsletter (January–February 1975): 137–143.

C.52   RATCLIFF, Carter.
'The Revival of Lithography'.
Architectural Digest (March–April 1971): 4, 68–77.

C.53 * RAUSCHENBERG, Robert.
Collage comment on *Stoned Moon*.
Studio International (December 1969): 246–247.

C.54   RENÉ, Denise, interviewed by Jean Clay.
Studio International (April 1968): 192–195.

C.55   RIVERS, Larry.
'Tatyana Grosman — There is Power in Obsession, and Finally it is Catching'.
Artnews (October 1982): 101–102.

C.56   ROSE, Barbara.
'The Graphic Work of Jasper Johns' (Parts 1 and 2).
Artforum (March 1970): 39–45; (September 1970): 65–74.

C.57 * ROSE, Barbara.
'The Airflow Multiples of Claes Oldenburg'.
Studio International (June 1970): 254–255.

C.58 * ROSIN, Mark.
'Pedigreed Prints'.
Harper's Bazaar (September 1971): 63.

C.59 * RUSSELL, John.
'A Connoisseur's Guide to the Fine Art of Print Collecting'.
New York Times, 22 June 1979, Section C, pp.1, 24.

C.60   SCHUYLER, James.
'Is There an American Print Revival? New York'.
Artnews (January 1962): 36, 37.

C.61   SELDIS, Henry J.
'New York's Grudging Tribute to Tamarind'.
Los Angeles Times Calendar, 4 May 1969, 43, 44.

C.62   SHESTACK, Alan.
'Jasper Johns: Reflections'.
Print Collector's Newsletter (January–February 1978): 172–174.

C.63   SMITH, Kathryn.
'June Wayne: Breaking the Stereotype'.
CURRÀNT (May–June–July 1976): 14–25.

C.64 * SOMMERS, John.
'The Acid-Tint Lithograph'.
The Tamarind Papers 7, no. 1 (Spring 1984): 24–28.

C.65 * STASIK, Andrew, ed.
American Prints and Printmaking 1956–1981 (25th anniversary issue).
Print Review 13, Pratt Graphics Center, 1981.

C.66   STASIK, Andrew, ed.
Prints U.S.A. 1982.
Print Review 15, Pratt Graphics Center, 1982.

C.67   TABAK, May Natalie.
'Tamarind Lithography Workshop' (Parts 1, 2 and 3).
Craft Horizons (October 1970): 28–33, 63; (December 1970): 50–53, 74–75; (February 1971): 34–37, 60.

C.68 * TOMKINS, Calvin.
'Profiles: The Moods of a Stone' [Tatyana Grosman].
New Yorker (7 June 1976): 42–76.

C.69   TOMKINS, Calvin.
'The Art World, Tatyana Grosman'.
New Yorker (9 August 1982): 82–86.

C.70   TOMKINS, Calvin.
'The Space Around Real Things' [Stella].
New Yorker (10 September 1984): 53–97.

C.71   WALDMAN, Diane.
'Color, Format and Abstract Art: An Interview with Kenneth Noland'.
Art in America (May–June 1977): 99–105.

C.72   WAYNE, June.
'The Male Artist as a Stereotypical Female'.
Art Journal (Summer 1973): 414–416.

C.73   WAYNE, June.
'The Creative Process: Artists, Carpenters, and the Flat Earth Society'.
Craft Horizons (October 1976): 30–31, 64–67.

C.74   WELLIVER, Neil.
'Albers on Albers'.
Artnews (January 1966): 48–51, 68.

C.75   WIGHT, Frederick S.
'Tamarind and the Art of the Lithograph'.
U.C.L.A. Art (1962–3): 7–9.

C.76 * YOUNG, Joseph E.
'Jasper Johns: An Appraisal'.
Art International (September 1969): 50–56.

C.77 * YOUNG, Joseph E.
'Claes Oldenburg at Gemini'.

Artist's Proof (1969): 44–52.

C.78 *YOUNG, Joseph E.
'Lichtenstein Printmaker'.
Art and Artists (March 1970): 50–53.

C.79 *YOUNG, Joseph E.
'Gemini Gallery, Los Angeles Exhibition'.
Art International (20 May 1971): 79.

C.80 *YOUNG, Joseph E.
'Jasper Johns' Lead-Relief Prints'.
Artist's Proof (1971): 36–38.

C.81 *YOUNG, Joseph E.
' "Pages" and "Fuses": An Extended View of
Robert Rauschenberg'.
Print Collector's Newsletter (May–June
1974): 25–30.

C.82 ZERNER, Henri.
'Universal Limited Art Editions'.
L'Oeil (December 1964): 36–43, 82.

Part D

Unpublished sources — interviews, letters and
manuscripts (all sources, including tape-recordings
of interviews, are housed in the archives of the
Australian National Gallery)

D.1   ADAMS, Clinton (Director of Tamarind
Institute).
Interviewed by Pat Gilmour, 30 September
1983, Albuquerque, New Mexico.

D.2   ADAMS, Clinton.
Letter to Pat Gilmour, 5 February 1985.

D.3   ALBERS, Josef (artist and teacher).
Artist's File.
Albuquerque, New Mexico: Tamarind
Institute and University of New Mexico,
1964–1971.

D.4   ALBERS, Josef.
Telephone conversation with Kenneth Tyler,
18 August 1966.

D.5   ALBERS, Josef.
Telephone conversation with Kenneth Tyler,
29 August 1966.

D.6   ALBERS, Josef.
Seven other telephone conversations with
Kenneth Tyler (1966).

D.7   ALBERS, Josef.
Telephone conversation with Kenneth Tyler,
3 September 1968 (i).

D.8   ALBERS, Josef.
Telephone conversation with Kenneth Tyler,
3 September 1968 (ii).

D.9   ALBERS, Josef; HOPKINS, Henry (Los
Angeles County Museum); and TYLER,
Kenneth E.
Three-way conversation.
New Haven, Connecticut (not dated but *c*.
June 1966).

D.10 ANTREASIAN, Garo Z. (artist, teacher and
Tamarind Lithography Workshop's first
master printer).
Interviewed by Pat Gilmour, 17 March 1984,
Albuquerque, New Mexico.

D.11 BROWN, Kathan (master printer and
founder, Crown Point Press).
Interviewed by Pat Gilmour, 22 September
1984, Minneapolis.

D.12 CLOSE, Chuck (artist).
Interviewed by Pat Gilmour, 18 September
1984, New York.

D.13 FELSEN, Sidney (director, Gemini G.E.L.).
Letter to Pat Gilmour, 25 January 1985.

D.14 FRANKENTHALER, Helen (artist).
Telephone interview with Pat Gilmour,
9 March 1983.

D.15 GOLDSTON, Bill (master printer, Universal
Limited Art Editions).
Interviewed by Pat Gilmour, 16 March 1983,
Long Island, New York.

D.16 HAMILTON, Richard (artist).
Interviewed by Pat Gilmour, 3 February
1983, Henley-on-Thames.

D.17 HOLLANDER, Irwin (artist and former master
printer, Hollander's Workshop).
Interviewed by Pat Gilmour, 28 September
1984, Brooklyn, New York.

D.18 KUSHNER, Robert (artist).
Interviewed by Pat Gilmour, 29 September
1984, New York.

D.19 LEMON, Jack (master printer, Landfall
Press).
Interviewed by Pat Gilmour, 4 October
1983, Chicago.

D.20 LIEBERMAN, William S. (Curator of
Contemporary Art, Metropolitan Museum of
Art, New York).
Telephone interview with Pat Gilmour,
September 1984.

D.21 LOZINGOT, Serge (master printer, Gemini
G.E.L.).
Interviewed by Pat Gilmour, 27 September
1983, Los Angeles.

D.22 PRATER, Christopher (master printer, Kelpra
Prints).
Interviewed by Pat Gilmour, 9 February
1983, London.

D.23 SANCHEZ, Maurice (master printer, Derrière
L'Etoile).
Interviewed by Pat Gilmour, 15 March 1983,
New York.

D.24 STELLA, Frank (artist).
Interviewed by Pat Gilmour, 26 September
1984, New York.

D.25 TYLER, Kenneth E. (founder and master
printer, Gemini G.E.L., and founder and
master printer, Tyler Graphics).
Interviewed by Pat Gilmour, 2 September
1984, Minneapolis.

D.26 TYLER, Kenneth E.
Interviewed by Pat Gilmour, 14, 15, 16
December 1984, Bedford Village.

D.27   TYLER, Kenneth E.
Interviewed by Pat Gilmour, January 1985,
Bedford Village.

D.28   TYLER, Kenneth E.
Interviewed by Michael Crichton, April 1971,
Los Angeles.

D.29   TYLER, Kenneth E.
'Notes and observations taken from Marcel
Durassier during his visit to Tamarind',
September 1963.

D.30   TYLER, Kenneth E.
Report to the National Endowment for the
Arts concerning an experimental research
and development grant [including a report by
Larry Hardy, paper consultant].
(A-04291-68-1-15), February 1969.

D.31   WAGSTAFF, Sam (former curator of the
Wadsworth Atheneum).
Interviewed by Pat Gilmour, 9 March 1983,
New York.

D.32   WAYNE, June (artist and founder of
Tamarind Lithography Workshop), and
HAMILTON, Ed (June Wayne's personal
printer).
Interviewed by Pat Gilmour, 26 September
1983, Los Angeles.

D.33   WAYNE, June.
Letter to Pat Gilmour, 21 December 1984.

D.34   WAYNE, June.
Letter to Pat Gilmour, 9 January 1985.

D.35   WAYNE, June.
Letter to Pat Gilmour, 28 January 1985.

CHECKLIST OF PREPARATORY DRAWINGS AND RARE PROOFS IN THE TYLER ARCHIVE IN THE AUSTRALIAN NATIONAL GALLERY

All measurements refer to sheet size unless indicated otherwise and are given in centimetres, height before width.

Josef ALBERS
Germany/United States   1888–1976
1973.852
Drawing related to the positioning of squares in the *Homage to the square* series.   1963
pencil, coloured pencil on graph paper
47.8 × 52.8 cm
inscribed 'for Ken my excellent helper / Josef Albers / × 28 1963'

1973.855
Diagram showing printing order for *White line squares I-XVI* (drawn by Ken Tyler).   February 1966
fibre-tipped pen, coloured pencil, ball-point pen
48.4 × 52.6 cm

1973.856
Diagram showing printing order and elements for *White line squares* (drawn by Ken Tyler).   February 1966
coloured pencil, fibre-tipped pen, ball-point pen on graph paper
35.6 × 43.2 cm

1973.854. A–B
Studies for *White line squares III, VI*.   1966
oil on card mounted on board, fibre-tipped pen, ball-point pen, pencil
48.4 × 52.6 cm

1973.853. A–E
Lay-out design for *White line squares II, V, VIII, IX, XIV*.   1966
collages of coloured paper on board
48.4 × 52.6 cm

1973.850.8
Preliminary drawing for *Embossed linear construction* project.   1965
pencil, fibre-tipped pen on Strathmore drawing paper
37.0 × 58.6 cm
working notes by Tyler (1968) in pencil

1973.850.1
Preliminary drawing for *Embossed linear construction 1–A*.   1965
pencil, fibre-tipped pen on Strathmore drawing paper
37.0 × 58.6 cm
working notes by Albers and Tyler in pencil

1973.850.2
Preliminary drawing for *Embossed linear construction 1–A*.   1969
fibre-tipped pen on drafting film
40.4 × 60.8 cm
working notes by Albers and Tyler in pencil, ball-point pen

1973.850.3
Photocopy of preliminary drawing for *Embossed linear construction 1–A*.   1969
37.0 × 58.4 cm
working notes by Albers and Tyler in pencil, ball-point pen

1973.850.4
Preliminary drawing for *Embossed linear construction 1–B*.   1965
fibre-tipped pen, pencil on drafting film
36.4 × 57.4 cm

1973.850.6
Photocopy of preliminary drawing for *Embossed linear construction 1–B*.   1969
36.6 × 58.4 cm
working notes by Albers and Tyler in ball-point pen, pencil

1973.850.7
Preliminary drawing for *Embossed linear construction 1–C*.   1965
pencil, fibre-tipped pen
37.0 × 58.6 cm
working notes by Tyler in pencil

1973.850.9
Preliminary drawing for *Embossed linear construction 1–D*.   1969
pencil, coloured pencil on vellum paper
36.6 × 58.6 cm
working notes by Albers and Tyler in pencil and ball-point pen

1973.850.11
Preliminary drawing for *Embossed linear construction 1–E*.   October 1968
fibre-tipped pen on drafting film
28.2 × 50.6 cm
working notes by Tyler in pencil

1973.850.10
Preliminary drawing for *Embossed linear construction 1–E and 1–F*.   1968
fibre-tipped pen on Strathmore drawing paper
58.4 × 73.6 cm

1973.850.5
Preliminary drawing for *Embossed linear
construction 1–F*.   1965
pencil, fibre-tipped pen on Strathmore drawing
paper
37.0 × 58.4 cm
working notes by Tyler in pencil

1973.850.12
Preliminary drawing for *Embossed linear
construction 1–F*.   1969
fibre-tipped pen on drafting film
31.2 × 52.0 cm
working notes by Tyler in pencil

1973.850.14
Preliminary drawing for *Embossed linear
construction 2–A*.   1964
fibre-tipped pen on Strathmore drawing paper
37.0 × 58.6 cm

1973.850.13
Photocopy of preliminary drawing for *Embossed
linear construction 2–A*.   1969
40.6 × 61.2 cm
working notes by Albers in ball-point pen

1973.850.15
Photocopy of preliminary drawing for *Embossed
linear construction 2–C*.   1969
39.0 × 61.2 cm
working notes by Albers and Tyler in pencil, ball-
point pen

1973.850.16
Photocopy of preliminary drawing for *Embossed
linear construction 2–D*.   1969
39.6 × 60.6 cm
working notes by Albers and Tyler in pencil, ball-
point pen

1973.851.4
Working proof for *Embossed linear construction
1–D*.   10 March 1969
embossing
51.2 × 66.2 cm
working notes by Albers and Tyler in ball-point pen,
coloured pencil

1973.851.9
Working proof for *Embossed linear construction
2–B*.   1969
embossing
51.2 × 66.4 cm
working notes by Albers and Tyler in pencil,
coloured pencil

1973.851.8
Working proof for *Embossed linear construction
2–C*.   1969
embossing
50.2 × 65.8 cm
working notes by Albers and Tyler in pencil,
coloured pencil

1973.851.11
Working proof for *Embossed linear construction
2–D*.   10 March 1969
embossing
51.2 × 66.2 cm
working notes by Albers and Tyler in ball-point pen,
coloured pencil

1973.847.1
Preliminary drawing for *White embossing on gray I*

(drawn by Albers and Ken and Kay Tyler).   1970
fibre-tipped pen on drafting film taped onto
embossed paper
51.0 × 66.2 cm
working notes by Albers in fibre-tipped pen, ball-
point pen, pencil

1973.848
Working proof for *White embossing on
gray I*.   1970–71
embossing
77.0 × 57.0 cm
working notes by Albers and Tyler in fibre-tipped
pen, ball-point pen, pencil

1973.847.2
Preliminary drawing for *White embossing on
gray II*.   1970
fibre-tipped pen on drafting film
33.0 × 49.8 cm
working notes by Albers and Tyler in ball-point pen,
pencil, fibre-tipped pen

1973.847.3
Preliminary drawing for *White embossing on
gray III*.   1970
fibre-tipped pen on drafting film
50.8 × 33.2 cm
working notes by Albers and Tyler in pencil,
coloured pencil, ball-point pen

1973.847.4
Preliminary drawing for *White embossing on
gray IV*.   1970
fibre-tipped pen on drafting film
61.2 × 40.6
working notes by Albers and Tyler in pencil, fibre-
tipped pen, ball-point pen

1973.847.5
Preliminary drawing for *White embossing on
gray V*.   1970
fibre-tipped pen on drafting film
45.4 × 39.0 cm
working notes by Albers and Tyler in pencil,
coloured pencil, ball-point pen

1973.847.6
Preliminary drawing for *White embossing on
gray VI*.   1970
fibre-tipped pen on drafting film
45.2 × 29.0 cm
working notes by Albers and Tyler in ball-point pen,
pencil

1973.847.7
Preliminary drawing for *White embossing on
gray VI*.   1967
fibre-tipped pen, pencil
58.6 × 36.8 cm
signed and dated — 'A67'

1973.847.8
Preliminary drawing for *White embossing on
gray VI*.   c.1970
fibre-tipped pen, pencil
73.6 × 58.4 cm

John ALTOON
United States   1925–1969
'G' refers to Gemini print numbers

1973.861
Study for G.109.   1965
lithograph, pastel
89.2 × 58.2 cm

1973.860
Study for G.108 for *About women*.   1965
colour lithograph, pastel
48.4 × 48.6 cm

1973.863
Study for G.110 for *About women*.   1965
colour lithograph, pastel
89.2 × 59.1 cm

1973.858
Study for G.139 for *About women*.   1965
colour lithograph, pastel
48.6 × 48.6 cm

1973.859
Study for G.142 for *About women*.   1965
colour lithograph, pastel
48.6 × 48.6 cm

1973.862
Study for G.143 for *About women*.   1965
colour lithograph, pastel
48.4 × 96.8 cm

1973.865.1
Study for G.136.   1965
lithograph, pastel
75.4 × 105.2 cm

1973.865.2
Study for G.136.   1965
lithograph, pastel
75.2 × 105.4 cm

1973.865.3
Study for G.136.   1965
lithograph, pastel
75.4 × 104.6 cm

Sam FRANCIS
United States   born 1923

1973.880
Study for *Spleen (yellow)*.   1971
colour lithograph without all printing elements,
watercolour, gouache
89.4 × 210.0 cm

David HOCKNEY
Great Britain   born 1937

1973.1048
Cancellation proof for *Rolf Nelson*.   12 June 1968
colour lithograph hand-coloured with watercolour
105.2 × 75.4 cm

1973.1044
Trial proof II for *Rain*.   1973
colour lithograph, screenprint
99.4 × 80.6 cm
inscribed 'for Ken'

1973.1046
Study for *Picture of a simple framed traditional nude
drawing*.   1966
colour lithograph, pencil
81.8 × 58.8 cm

1973.1043
Cancellation proof for *Henry and
Christopher*.   1967
lithograph hand-coloured with watercolour
56.8 × 75.8 cm

1973.1042
Right to print proof for *Henry and*

Christopher.   1967
lithograph hand-coloured with watercolour, collage
57.0 × 76.4 cm

1973.1047
Henry and Christopher.   1967
(edition 14/15)
lithograph hand-coloured with watercolour without
collage element
57.2 × 76.6 cm

1973.1041
Study for *Snow*.   1973
watercolour, gouache, coloured pencil
89.0 × 75.0 cm
inscribed 'for Ken with much love'

1973.1045
Working proof for *Picture of Melrose Avenue in
ornate gold frame*.   1965
colour lithograph without all printing elements
76.8 × 56.4 cm
inscribed 'for Ken with love xxxx'

Jasper JOHNS
United States   born 1930

1973.1054
Cancellation proof for *Gray alphabets* (1/2).   1968
lithograph
152.4 × 106.6 cm

1973.1053
Trial proof for *Good time Charley II* (2/2 trial proof
4).   1971
colour lithograph
121.8 × 86.2 cm
inscribed 'for Ken'

1973.882
*Fragment according to what — leg
and chair* (1971).   1971
collage of photograph and paper, oil-paint, pencil,
brush and ink, powdered graphite, fibre-tipped pen
on cardboard
76.2 × 89.0 cm
inscribed 'for Ken Tyler'

Roy LICHTENSTEIN
United States   born 1923

1974.131
Preliminary drawing for *Haystack series*.   *c*.1969
fibre-tipped pen, pencil
63.2 × 82.3 cm
inscribed 'To Kay and Ken with love — Roy'

1973.896
Study for *Bull head I*.   1972
lithograph, fibre-tipped pen, pencil, collage of
painted paper on board
57.2 × 76.3 cm

Man RAY
United States   1890–1976

1973.1149
Study for *Hands*.   1966
gelatin silver photograph mounted on card
photograph: 50.5 × 40.5 cm

Claes OLDENBURG
United States   born 1929

1973.1132

Study for *Icebag*.   1970
one-colour lithograph
91.3 × 66.0 cm

Robert RAUSCHENBERG
United States   born 1925

1973.925
Cancellation proof for *Test stone 5A* (2nd
state).   1967
from the *Booster and seven studies* series
colour lithograph with one additional colour
63.6 × 83.8 cm
inscribed 'cancellation for Ken — love 67 — Bob'

1973.912
Trial proof II for *Horsefeathers thirteen I*.   1972
from the *Horsefeathers thirteen* series
colour offset photo-lithograph, collage of magazine
and paper pieces, embossing, colour screenprint,
pochoir, gloss varnish
71.4 × 57.0 cm
inscribed 'For Ken'

1973.945
Trial proof for *Sky garden* (3C 5/6).   1969
from the *Stoned moon* series
lithograph, screenprint
226.2 × 106.7 cm
inscribed 'For Ken Tyler'

Frank STELLA
United States   born 1936

1973.955.3
Colour trial proof for *Star
of Persia I*.   1967
colour lithograph on graph paper
66.0 × 78.6 cm

1973.955.4
Preliminary drawing/proof for *Star
of Persia II*.   1967
colour lithograph, fibre-tipped pen
68.5 × 81.2 cm

1973.954.2
Study for *Star of Persia* prints.   1967
lithograph on graph paper
66.0 × 81.2 cm

1973.955.5
Study for *Star of Persia* prints.   1967
lithograph on graph paper
92.6 × 66.0 cm

1973.954.2
Irving Blum memorial edition (state proof X).   1967
lithograph on graph paper
66.0 × 81.2 cm

1973.947.8
Marriage of reason and squalor (state I).   1967
from *Black series I*
lithograph without second colour
39.0 × 55.8 cm

1973.959
Study for *Bonne Bay*.   1970
gouache, lithograph on paper mounted on board
82.6 × 164.4 cm

1973.958.A–B
Drawings made after *Gavotte*.   1967
recto: lithographic crayon, pencil drawing
verso: pencil line drawing
38.2 × 53.4 cm
inscribed recto l.r. 'for Ken Tyler'

INDEX